FULLY ALIVE

FULLY ALIVE

The Process of Loving

DAVID FORRESTER

DARTON · LONGMAN + TODD

First published in 2001 by
Darton, Longman and Todd Ltd
1 Spencer Court
140-142 Wandsworth High Street
London SW18 4JJ

© 2001 David Forrester

ISBN 0-232-52407-6

Unless otherwise stated the Scripture quotations in this publication
are taken from The Jerusalem Bible, published and copyright
1966, 1967 and 1968 by Darton, Longman and Todd Ltd and
Doubleday & Co. Inc.

Extract from *Armada* by Brian Patten, published by HarperCollins
(Flamingo), 1996, is used by kind permission of the author.

A catalogue record for this book is available from the British
Library.

Designed by Sandie Boccacci
Phototypeset in 11.25/16pt Sabon by Intype London Ltd
Printed and bound in Great Britain by Page Bros, Norwich

CONTENTS

CONTENTS

PREFACE

Saint Irenaeus (*c.* 130–*c.* 200), Bishop of Lyons and the first great Catholic theologian, was of the view that 'The glory of God is a human being fully alive.' This small book is an attempt to discuss how each of us might become more fully alive.

Irenaeus, whose name means 'peace', was born at Smyrna in Asia Minor, and as a young man had sat at the feet of Polycarp, an intimate of St John, the disciple of Jesus and friend of St Ignatius, the third Bishop of Antioch after St Peter. Down the ages, Polycarp has been revered not only on account of his apostolic connections, but because of his tenderness and steadfastness in the face of persecution. He died a martyr at the age of eighty-six.

Irenaeus acquired from Polycarp not only his knowledge of the Christian faith, especially its apostolic vocabulary and theological convictions, but seemingly his gentleness and humility. Although, for example, he wrote against heretics, Irenaeus interceded with the pope on behalf of the Gnostics. Above all, he was completely committed to convincing others of the pivotal role of Jesus as the exponent of our purpose and destiny. He expressed this in the deceptively simple formula that Jesus, God's Word, 'on account of his measureless love became what we are that he might make us in the end what he is.'

At the same time as he was a profound thinker, Irenaeus was also a practical man and never separated theology from everyday life. It was due to Irenaeus more than anyone else that Christianity became securely rooted in southern France.

In the quest of discovering how we might all become more fully alive and ultimately more Christ-like, I have tried to root my explorations in the ordinary human experiences of everyday life. In an opening chapter I have endeavoured to reach conclusions as to the nature of Christian love. Then I have examined such fundamental aspects of Christian life as prayer, forgiveness, conversion, community and compassion in the context of love. Following this I have considered the saints as icons of love, or those who became most fully alive through loving. In a further chapter I have attempted to indicate how Christian marriage is ideally an image of love and finally how death and bereavement are testing experiences of love.

In writing this book I am conscious of how much I owe in the way of ideas and friendship to countless people. This is particularly true of the late Fr Michael Hollings who first taught me the value of prayer, of the people whom I served in different parishes, 1972–90, and the many Catholic students at Oxford during my tenure as Catholic Chaplain to the university, 1990–6. Special thanks are due to Teresa de Bertodano who skilfully took the scalpel to the original version of this book, and to Alastair Land with whom I discussed so many of its contents. I am also grateful to other masters and pupils currently at Eton College.

DAVID FORRESTER
Catholic Chaplain
Eton College

ONE

THE PROCESS OF LOVING

OBSTACLES OF LOVE

Not long ago, a friend of mine went on a retreat to a monastery for the first time in his life. After only a day and a half, however, he left. He could not bear the silence of the place. He hadn't realised that the monks only spoke when it was absolutely necessary, so the only sounds he heard indoors were the monastery bell and the singing of the monks in church. The silence frightened him. He had never previously appreciated how much noise featured in his life.

At home my friend experienced the perpetual sound of the radio and television, the phone, the doorbell, the voice of his wife and the continual chatter and laughter, sometimes crying, of his three children. The noise of traffic outside the house was another constant feature, as was the sound above of aircraft and, when the wind was in the right direction, the rattle of passing trains. Outdoors at the monastery, apart from the bell summoning the monks to prayer, the only sounds were those of the wind in the trees, the cry of birds and, in the distance, the sea.

Without human noises my friend felt as though he was in a vacuum. He became alarmed for it seemed unnatural to be so much on his own, especially on his own with God. Without distractions he was frightened. Even so, and although he fled, he wondered if he had ever before actually tried to listen to God. Until then he had lived in an environment which seemed to conspire to prevent him listening to anyone, including God.

Before leaving the monastery he spoke to the guest master about how he felt and the monk was sympathetic. The monk told him that was how he had felt when he had first come to the monastery, but that gradually it had become easier to live in the silence. He said that eventually the monastery became less a place where there was an absence of noise and much more a place in which he could hear God and learn his will, not least in regard to other people.

Noise is not the only barrier we experience between ourselves and God, and ourselves and other people. The kind of society in which we live often militates against our encountering and communicating with God and others. Small wonder then that, cut off from the author of life, we find it hard to discover the meaning of life, let alone how we may most fruitfully live our lives.

We live in a society increasingly indifferent to spiritual concerns and one in which more and more issues such as nationalism, increasing population, unemployment, racism, feminism and ecology, to name just a few, are not so much explored as fought over, in which emphasis is placed on acquisitiveness and competition, and in which vast social changes are taking place almost every day. Was there ever a time previously when the media and technological changes such as computerization exercised such influence in our lives? Who can recall when so much time and energy was put by others into considering us simply as consumers and so much money lavished on marketing, advertising and image building? Immense changes in social attitudes towards such things as cohabitation, divorce, one-parent families, abortion, embryo experimentation and euthanasia are also afoot. On the world stage we are seeing vast political changes such as those which have already taken place in South Africa and Eastern Europe, especially Russia. At the same time, there is an increasing number of civil and international wars, and with them a rise in the numbers of refugees as well as unprecedented waves of poverty and disease striking populations in the Third World. And yet, like the Christian message itself, the fundamental needs of human beings for such things as self-knowledge, awareness of the transcendent, understanding of eternal truths, intimacy, love and so on do not alter. Not all barriers against fulfilling our needs and achieving authentic happiness are external; often we erect them within ourselves through fear.

When it comes to revealing our true selves to others for example, what are we frightened of? Could it be that we fear our 'interior wilderness' will come into view? Are we frightened because we might be revealed as someone who believes he or she is not as beautiful or attractive as others; as someone who fears they're not very intelligent or as bright as others; as someone frightened of their feelings; as someone worried about being rejected by others, especially by those we admire; as someone who feels inferior to others; and as someone different from how others imagine or believe us to be and therefore a potential object of derision? Haven't we all at some time encountered people who were never truly honest with their friends for fear of losing them, or others who have such a poor self-image that they go on to act out roles, instead of being their real selves?

A few years ago a young man asked if he might bring his girlfriend to see me in connection with her having recently attempted suicide. It turned out that the girl in question had a weight problem and to enable her to keep a brave face on things had adopted the role of a clown among her friends and associates. Eventually, of course, no one took her seriously about anything, so she began to doubt everything about herself from her intellectual ability to her real talent as a musician. By then she had also become tired of playing the clown and the strain of pretending was such that she took an overdose. When she recovered consciousness in hospital, she was startled to see an exceptionally beautiful girl in the next bed who had deliberately cut her wrists. Only then did it dawn on her that external appearance is not everything. From then on she ceased regarding her weight as a problem and in this attitude she was immensely assisted by the love she was given by her boyfriend.

For the fact is that love, defined as willing the good of another, and being accepted as one truly is, warts and all, is the cure for most if not all our weaknesses. Indeed, this kind of love is also vital to our spiritual lives; as the Dominican priest Gerald Vann put it succinctly years ago, 'Just as sex without love is spiritually sterile, so life without love is sterile.'

This, of course, is why friendship or the sharing of what is most personal and intimate about oneself with another is so important. To be able to speak freely of one's weaknesses and failings without the fear of being judged, and to share one's most hidden thoughts with another without the possibility of being derided, is a precious gift. When friendship is combined with love then the combination is momentous, as Thomas Merton has testified.

Love not only prefers the good of another to my

own, but it does not even compare the two. It has only one good: that of the beloved, which is, at the same time, my own. Love shares the good with another not by dividing it with him, but by identifying itself with him so that his good becomes my own . . . Love seeks its whole good in the good of the beloved, so to divide that good would be to diminish love . . . Love seeks one thing only: the good of the beloved.

(*No Man Is An Island*)

Not long ago I was visited by two students who were in love. The world was their oyster as we say and they were immensely happy. Both of them were bright and gifted, both impressive as individuals and even more as a pair. Both shared a remarkable sense of humour and were unusually mature. There was nothing silly or sloppy about their relationship, nothing in it which in the least resembled something out of a sentimental novel. Their relationship indeed was founded on reality and truth, for although they sometimes disagreed with each other, had fights and fell out, their unselfish love was stronger than any temporary disagreement and enabled them to be reconciled.

Then shortly after they had been to see me, the girl had a terrible accident. She fell from the sixth floor of a building and was killed. Obviously her boyfriend was numb with grief. But though nothing will ever be the same again for him amid his pain, he was determined to hold fast to all that had been good in their relationship. It was as though parts of him which he had previously not known existed were brought into being by his suffering. Their love for each other proved stronger than death.

Another barrier to our finding fulfilment and true happiness is often our pride. Legend has it that St Francis of Assisi once sent his followers out into the world with the instruction, 'Go out and preach the Good News' and then he added, 'Use words only if necessary.' In saying this, Francis appreciated that for many people words are the equivalent of riches and the source of their wealth. For such people riches consist not in such obvious things as money, property, investments and material objects, but in ideas, theories, beliefs, qualifications, ambitions and plans, all expressed in words. The danger is that they may lead just as much as obvious riches to pride and false notions of autonomy.

Individuals endowed with a gift for words have in their possession a double-edged sword. Either they may use such a gift in the service of others or become enamoured with their talent. This is the danger of which Francis of Assisi was aware, particularly when an individual might be tempted to credit such a talent to his or her own efforts, instead of viewing it as a gift from God. As a student for the priesthood with a talent for preaching was once told by his tutor, 'You have a great gift, but don't fall in love with it!' An additional danger for such a student was that he might have gone on to confuse cleverness, acquired through the skilled use of words, with wisdom. Instead, because of the advice from his tutor he learnt to value wisdom. He made his own the description of wisdom in the Bible:

... I held riches as nothing,
I reckoned no priceless stone to be her peer,
for compared with her, all gold is a pinch of sand,
and beside her silver ranks as mud.

(Book of Wisdom 7:8-9)

As a young newly appointed tutor at Oxford was once advised by the head of his college, 'Don't try to be clever here. Here we are all clever. Try to be wise.' Furthermore, the merely clever use of words often only serves to mislead others and render them akin to the character, Austin Brierley, in David Lodge's novel *How Far Can You Go?* (Penguin 1981). Poor Austin Brierley discovered in the face of so many conflicting ideologies cleverly presented to him at university that his head became 'a buzzing hive of awakened but directionless ideas.'

There was Freud who said that we must acknowledge our own repressed desires, and Jung who said that we must recognize our archetypal patterning, and Marx who said we must join the class struggle and Marshall McLuhan who said we must watch more television.

There was Sartre who said that man was absurd
though free and Skinner who said he was a bundle
of conditioned reflexes and Chomsky who said
he was a sentence-generating organism . . .

Each book that Austin read seemed to him
totally persuasive at the time, but they couldn't all
be right. And which were most easily reconcilable
with faith in God? For that matter, what was
God?

Kant said he was the essential presupposition
of moral action, Bishop Robinson said he was the
ground of our being, and Teilhard de Chardin
said he was the Omega Point. Wittgenstein said,
whereof we cannot speak, thereof we must remain
silent.

Those who have been blessed with the gift for words
but who take undue pride in their ability to use them,
would do well to read again the story of the rich
young man in the Bible, who approached Jesus and
asked what he should do to inherit eternal life. Having
ascertained that the young man was faithful in keeping
the Ten Commandments,

Jesus looked steadily at him and loved him, and
he said, 'There is one thing you lack. Go and sell
everything you own and give the money to the
poor, and you will have treasure in heaven; then
come, follow me.' But his face fell at these words
and he went away sad, for he was a man of great
wealth. (Mark 10:21-2)

This was an encounter paralleled in the life of Francis of Assisi. Francis also understood that riches in the form of words, when overestimated, could just as easily prevent one following Jesus and discovering fulfilment as any amount of material wealth. It is rumoured that when Francis met St Dominic, they didn't speak a word but simply embraced and went their separate ways. Words were superfluous.

But that still leaves unanswered the question of how one begins this process of loving and being loved by which we are not only healed but enabled to become more fully alive.

STEPS IN THE PROCESS OF LOVE

The first step in this process of loving and being loved is to risk appearing 'naked' or open as it were, to risk revealing our true selves to those we are brave enough to trust. Even so, this should only be done after a period and process of discernment. Such an authority on human relationships as Aelred of Rievaulx once told his sister that her heart had to be a kind of Noah's ark in which there was room for all in need, but Aelred recognised that not everyone we love is suitable for friendship. He considered it difficult, for example, to become friends with people who are by nature irascible, unstable, suspicious or talkative, and he maintained that all friendships should result from a sensible period of probation.

Secondly, we should not be frightened of our feelings for as the late Cardinal Basil Hume, when Abbot of Ampleforth, told his monks:

> You must never be frightened of your affections. If you did not feel drawn to some persons more than to others you would, I think, be a very odd human being. That is the first thing – never be frightened or surprised. Secondly, remember that you cannot ignore your emotions, as if they did not exist ... Thirdly, these cannot be stifled: it is dangerous to try to stifle them, to extinguish them, to live as if they were not there. They are part of you ... We have to acquire a freedom in our relationship with others – an ease – but going with it must be a control ... And by control I mean a realisation of where the limits lie. "Yes" to others spells freedom and ease; "No" to oneself, control. It is in this area that the key lies.
>
> (*Searching for God*, St Bede's Publications, 2000)

Then we have to be genuine in our interest in the other, whether it be another human being or even God. Pretence is out, even though T.S. Eliot truthfully said that 'Humankind cannot bear very much reality.' It is possible of course that in relation to another human being we shall be rebuffed, but never in relation to God. On the other hand, can there ever be real growth without pain? Mother Teresa once remarked that 'I have found the paradox that if I love until it hurts, then there is no hurt, but only more love.'

At all times we must also remember that we are made in the image of God who is love and are individually unique. As Martin Buber, quoting Yechiel Mikhal, remarked:

> Every person born into this world represents something new, something that never existed before, something original and unique. It is the duty of everyone ... to know and consider that he or she is unique in the world, that there has never been anyone like him or her, for if there had been someone like him or her, there would have been no need for him or her to be in the world ... Everyone's foremost task is the actualization of his or her unique, unprecedented and never-returning potentialities.
>
> (*Hasidism and Modern Man*, Humanities, 1988)

At the same time we must beware of the enemies of love such as infidelity, jealousy, possessiveness, suspicion, untruthfulness, gossip and anger. Confucius once said that 'To love a thing means wanting it to live.' We must never suffocate those we love, but instead give them space, freedom, time and above all trust.

A father was once asked by one of his sons when young if he would teach him to play cricket. He was delighted by such a request and for the next few weeks gladly gave up his afternoons to instructing his small son in everything he knew about the art of cricket; the basic rules of batting, bowling and fielding.

Then one afternoon, as he observed his young son coming towards him through the house swinging his bat, he assumed that it was time for their regular practice together and he also moved to pick up his own bat and join his son. That particular afternoon, however, the boy shouted that he was off to play with his friends instead, and his father had to be content with watching his son continue walking through the house and away to join his friends.

At first the father was taken aback, if not exactly devastated. He had so enjoyed playing cricket with his son that he hadn't imagined that one day his son would reach the stage of no longer needing him. After his initial reaction of shock and hurt, he realised how important it was for his son's development to let him go, as it were, and not to be possessive of him. The wisdom of letting go and not being possessive is illustrated in the lines of the poem by C. Day Lewis:

> Self-hood begins with a walking away,
> And love is proved in the letting go.
>> ('Walking Away' in *The Gate*,
>> Jonathan Cape, 1962)

This is a truth which we must all follow in relationships of love. For when love is authentic, it inevitably involves sacrifice, and when we genuinely love we want what is best for the other person, not ourselves.

But in any case, didn't Jesus himself warn us that love inevitably involves sacrifice? He said, 'If anyone wants to be a follower of mine, let him renounce himself and take up his cross every day and follow me' (Matthew 16:24).

This dimension of sacrifice was brought forcibly home to me a few years ago during a visit to a priests' convention in North America. On one occasion and as part of the convention, the four hundred priests present attended a service led by the local bishop in a nearby cathedral. For many of us the bishop's sermon proved at first to be irrelevant and boring, but then he suddenly woke us up by ceasing to preach and instead pointing to another bishop sitting quietly opposite him. 'That bishop there,' he said, 'has come from Guatemala, speaks no English and has asked me to appeal to you.' He then went on to give statistics about his friend's diocese and in particular about how many priests, nuns and catechists there had either disappeared, been tortured or shot. He then called for volunteers from among us to replace the priests who had been killed. Those of us present were immediately put on the spot. Which among us would have the courage and degree of commitment necessary to answer such a call? Which of us would be prepared to sacrifice our comfortable way of life in the name of love? Four priests then stepped forward, including one who was sitting next to me. It was an occasion I shall never forget.

Then, in this process of loving we must remember

that genuine love involves dialogue accompanied by real concern for the other person, or as Martin Buber expressed it: 'Dialogue, without real outgoing to the other, reaching out to the other, accompanying the other; love which remains within itself, this is called Lucifer.'

On the other hand, if our love involves true dialogue we shall lose our fear, and in being accepted we shall lose our sense of inferiority. We shall then begin to value ourselves, which is a necessary preliminary to any love for another, including God. For as Jürgen Moltmann succinctly puts it:

> Love for God's creation is love for his works. Love for human beings is love of his image. Direct love of God's image is a love of the self. This is why, according to Bernard of Clairvaux, love of our neighbour begins with love of ourselves: love thy neighbour as thyself, not vice versa. Love of the self as love of God's image in oneself is a step towards the love of God, and part of it.
>
> (*Experiences of God*)

St Bernard's contemporary, Aelred of Rievaulx, was equally of the view that 'A man who does not love himself cannot possibly love another, for the love he offers his neighbour must be framed on the kind of love he has for himself.'

In the Gospel of St Matthew there is the account of John the Baptist sending two of his disciples to discover whether or not Jesus is the Messiah whom John had preached about. In reply to their question, Jesus says neither Yes nor No, but tells them to return to John and inform him what they have seen, namely that 'the blind see again, the lame walk, the lepers are cleansed and the deaf hear, the dead are raised to life, the Good News is proclaimed' (Matthew 11:4-5). In other words, they witnessed the Messiah going about his own appropriate business, putting love into action and demonstrating the difference between authentic and false love, reality and romance.

Some time ago I had lunch with a friend in London who informed me that two days previously he had attended a book sale. At the latter he was immensely taken with the beauty of a girl behind one of the bookstalls whom he heard someone call Joanne. He was also present when Joanne cut her finger on the edge of a book wrapped in cellophane.

All the way home my friend could not rid his mind of this pretty girl, Joanne, so he called at a chemist shop, bought some Band-aid, hailed a taxi and sent the taxi driver back to the book fair with the instructions to find a girl called Joanne, hand her the Band-aid for her cut finger, and give her a note containing his telephone number and an invitation to supper one evening.

To his delight, Joanne called back, remarked on the originality and practicality of his approach which she considered a change from flowers, and accepted his invitation to dinner.

This is a true story and not something from an

advertisement on television. It illustrates how we can be immediately attracted to someone without knowing anything about them. We are drawn by their looks, their smile, how they dress, how they carry themselves and how they move. Yet one cannot call this love, nor is my friend's romantic approach sheer lust. It is simply a form of yearning which indeed may be at least an ingredient of love, if it is a yearning to make the other person happy.

It is possible that my friend who went to the book fair will come eventually to love the girl, Joanne. But it is one thing and possibly exhilarating to be in the presence of someone to whom one is attracted. It is quite another thing, however, to feel totally free, totally at ease, totally secure, in their presence and to know, without asking, their likes and dislikes, to enjoy their humour, to feel incomplete when separated from them, and from time to time to be one with them in silence, without worry. All these things come as the result of hard work and they take time. The hard work includes such things as showing interest in the concerns of the other, ensuring that their wishes are taken into account, expressing appreciation of them, and being willing to speak the truth, even when it hurts.

When it comes to loving God, the process we need to follow is similar. After all, we should not seek to behave in one way with our neighbour and in another with God, although we should never forget that when it comes to knowing God the stakes are different in kind and considerably higher. This is indicated in that section of John's Gospel, the High Priestly Prayer, where Jesus praying to his Father says, 'And eternal life is this: to know you, the only true God, and Jesus Christ whom you have sent' (John 17:3).

Most obviously we love God by giving him time and space in our lives, by cultivating his presence through study of the Scriptures and frequenting the sacraments, by engaging in prayer with him, endeavouring to do what he wills, expressing thanks and praise, seeking his forgiveness and, not least, by giving him glory through being fully alive.

Our love either for God or another human being must also be personal and concrete. It isn't enough to love in the name of an abstraction such as society, the human race, the common good or even community. For as John Henry Newman stated, the human heart is commonly reached not through reason but through the imagination, by means of direct impressions. According to Newman, 'Persons influence us, voices melt us, looks subdue us, deeds inflame us.' And as he rightly concludes, 'Many a man will live upon a dogma: no man will be a martyr for a conclusion' (*Grammar of Assent*).

A former Benedictine abbot now dead, Dominic Gaisford of Worth Abbey, was of the opinion that 'if I am to become truly alive, truly human, I need to love, to learn how to love and be loved, in relation both to God and to people.' He added that he was equally convinced that such love had to be rooted and grounded in his relationship with God, otherwise it would veer towards what he termed the fickle, the shallow and the predominantly physical; something which he declared would cause in the end as much, possibly more, frustration and sense of unfulfilment than celibacy can do (*A Touch of God*). It is for this reason that in the next chapter we shall examine the place of prayer in the process of becoming fully alive.

Finally, as Jesus taught his disciples when he said that 'A man can have no greater love than to lay down his life for his friends' (John 15:13), and as he put this truth into practice on the cross, authentic love necessarily involves self-sacrifice.

As is often pointed out to visitors to Eton College Chapel, just inside the main entrance there hangs an old faded French flag, the tricolour. It has been hanging there since 1915, when it was rescued from behind the German trenches during the First World War by a former boy of the school, George Fletcher.

Like so many others, George Fletcher had immediately volunteered for the army when war broke out and had been despatched to the trenches in France. About a year later he was moved to a different part of the front and noticed a French flag flying from a tree behind the German lines. It had been captured by the Germans and deliberately hung there to taunt and humiliate the French. On behalf of his French friends and allies, Fletcher was determined to retrieve their honour. One night, not long after first spotting the flag, Fletcher crawled across no man's land, went behind the enemy lines, recovered the tricolour, and returned to his own trenches. For this the French soldiers held him in high esteem. Two days later he was shot dead by a sniper and the flag was sent by the French to Eton where it has been hanging ever since. To what extent would we risk our lives for our friends?

TWO

PRAYER: A PART
OF THE PROCESS OF
LOVING

THE NEED TO PERSEVERE

One Sunday evening a few years ago, I had an unfortunate experience. Halfway through preaching a sermon I was interrupted by a woman who was drunk and who is indeed an alcoholic and a beggar. She stood up, approached the lectern, shouted abuse, began singing, heckled whenever I said anything, and laughed in a demonic fashion.

I asked her to sit down, I offered to listen to her and discuss with her whatever she liked after the service, but she refused adamantly. Then she did sit down, but continued interrupting. I began to get impatient, even angry inside, but realised the importance of keeping calm, not least because the congregation of about two hundred students were watching keenly to see how I would handle the situation. Then I deliberately changed tactics and asked how her son was. She promptly burst into tears. Apparently he was in hospital suffering from pneumonia, having slept outdoors in bitterly cold weather. He too is what we euphemistically call 'a man of the road'.

At that point, two nuns got up and attempted to escort the woman out of the church, an action she did not appreciate and which caused her to get even more abusive. It also made the students uneasy and I stopped the nuns from proceeding. The woman then moved among the choir and the musicians, coming across a student called Danny and on learning his name commenced singing 'Oh, Danny Boy' at the top of her voice. Finally at the consecration she declared we were all hypocrites and left.

This was not an altogether unusual experience. Aggressive beggars, homeless people, alcoholics, the unemployed, mentally handicapped people, the deprived and lately refugees from Eastern Europe all seem to be on the increase in our streets. Young people in particular are constantly asking me how they should behave and react in the face of this needy but increasingly militant army of angry human beings, each made in the image of God. Often they are troubled because they are made to feel guilty about their own privileged position in comparison with people on our streets. They are also aware that Christ aligned himself with such poor during his life on earth.

> Into this world, this demented inn, in which there is absolutely no room for Him at all, Christ has come uninvited. But because He cannot be at home in it, because He is out of place in it, His place is with those for whom there is no room. His place is with those who do not belong, who are rejected by power because they are regarded as weak, those who are discredited, who are denied the status of persons, (those unjustly accused and condemned). With those for whom there is no room, Christ is present in the world. He is mysteriously present in those for whom there seems to be nothing but the world at its worst . . . It is in these that He hides himself, for whom there is no room.
>
> (Thomas Merton, *Raids on the Unspeakable*, Burns and Oates, 1977)

In the first instance, I usually tell young people to become what we call 'street-wise', to behave prudently, and to be realistic in their response to demands for assistance. Then, despite distressing experiences, I remind them of St Paul's dictum that they should not give up if trials come and that they should keep on praying.

I give them this advice because prayer is not something pious, remote from earthly concerns, something pristine, precious or hygienic, but is dialogue with a God who is passionately interested in everything that occurs in our lives. In that sense prayer is as vital to our daily lives as eating, drinking, sleeping and indeed breathing. If we are failing to pray, we are not fully alive. We shall also never know what it means to be fulfilled, unless we seek to become so from our experience of a vibrant, dynamic and vital relationship with God, deeply rooted in prayer. Few things indeed are actually more important than prayer because everything in our lives, now and ultimately, hangs on the nature of our relationship with God. And this, in its turn, is determined by the quality of our prayer-lives.

When teaching his disciples about the end of the world, Jesus advised them to 'Stay awake, praying at all times for the strength to survive all that is going to happen' (Luke 21:36). If the Son of God tells us that is the best way to prepare for his return, it behoves us at least to try and understand what prayer is. Moreover, if St Paul tells us not to give up when trials come and to keep on praying, prayer must surely be viewed as something significant and not as something trivial or effete. When we love someone deeply we are prepared to sweat blood if necessary to deepen the relationship between us. Should we spend less effort on prayer when it is the way in which we relate with our Creator and Saviour, who alone is most able to direct our path and teach us how to behave in all the situations we may find ourselves?

For that reason we should begin by giving a specific amount of time to God in prayer every day and stick to it, no matter what. Furthermore we should pray as we are, not in imitation of someone else, no matter how impressive they may be. Then we should endeavour to pray at all times, not just during those periods we have laid aside for the purpose. We should utilise in particular all those times we now waste; when we grow impatient in a bus queue or traffic jam, standing in line at the cash till at the supermarket, when walking from place A to place B, when sitting in the doctor's surgery or the local pub waiting for a friend to turn up, travelling on a bus or train, lying in bed in the morning before getting up and so on.

When Pope John Paul II addressed young people during his visit to Britain he said:

> In Jesus, whom you get to know in prayer, your dreams for justice and your dreams for peace become more definite and look for practical applications ... Through contact with Jesus in prayer, you gain a sense of mission that nothing can dull ... In union with Jesus in prayer, you will discover more fully the needs of your brothers and sisters. You will appreciate more keenly the pain and suffering that burden the hearts of countless people ... Through prayer you will receive the strength to resist the spirit of the

world. You will receive the power to show compassion to every human being – just as Jesus did ... It is my hope today, as I return to Rome, that you will remember why I came among you. And as long as the memory of this visit lasts, may it be recorded that I, John Paul II, came to Britain to call you to Christ, to invite you to pray!

Such is the importance of prayer that it is useful to recall how Jesus himself regularly made time for prayer in his daily life, suggesting that it was from prayer that he derived the strength to face the frequently exhausting pressures and calls upon his time. Mention is made in all the Gospels of his allotment of time for prayer, whether in the early morning, or 'after sending the crowds away' when Jesus went up into the hills to pray following the first miracle of the loaves and fishes (Matthew 14:13ff.). It is also clear that he made his first priority in prayer the need to do the will of his Father. In the Garden of Gethsemane this was his basic prayer. 'My Father,' he said, 'if it is possible, let this cup pass me by. Nevertheless, let it be as you, not I, would have it' (Matthew 26:39). Almost as firmly Jesus emphasised in his teaching on prayer the place of humility and self-effacement.

'Two men went up to the Temple to pray, one a Pharisee, the other a tax collector. The Pharisee stood there and said this prayer to himself, "I thank you, God, that I am not grasping, unjust, adulterous like the rest of mankind, and particularly that I am not like this tax collector here. I fast twice a week; pay tithes on all I get." The tax collector stood some distance away, not daring even to raise his eyes to heaven; but beat his breast and said, "God, be merciful to me, a sinner." This man, I tell you, went home at rights with God; the other did not. For everyone who exalts himself will be humbled, but the man who humbles himself will be exalted.' (Luke 18:9-14)

Some years ago I helped to organise a conference in Oxford on the nineteenth-century writer and theologian Cardinal John Henry Newman, at which the speakers were international scholars. Before the conference began there was a reception to which distinguished people from all walks of life, such as politicians, diplomats, bishops, and famous academics, had been invited.

Even though I was busy helping to run the conference, I couldn't help observing those present who *wanted* to be seen and heard, those who sought the limelight and the television cameras, and those who put on a display in order to attract attention. And then I noticed an elderly man, a priest called Stephen Dessain, standing quietly alone, minding his own business, not being unsociable but quite obviously not seeking or needing to be the centre of things. He turned out actually to be the leading authority in the world at that time on the conference topic. Even so, after he had delivered his paper and received rapturous applause from the audience, I watched him slip away to catch his train, unseen by anyone but myself.

Because that man was so patently the opposite of everything the Pharisee mentioned above stood for, in other words because he was so humble, I sought his friendship over the next few years and discovered that nothing ever moved him quite so much as prayer. Indeed the only thing which ever upset him was anyone failing to take the subject of prayer seriously. He died not too long ago singing the Gloria as he was saying Mass which struck me as the most appropriate way for such a humble man to die.

THE DIFFERENT TYPES OF PRAYER

If therefore we are sincerely seeking to learn how to serve our neighbour and thereby become both happy and fully alive, it makes sense to take prayer seriously as well as learn the many different types of prayer and ways of praying. It may be useful, but not essential, to categorise these as some have done into the three 'levels' of prayer, known as purification, illumination and union, before one reaches complete unity of heart and mind with God. The chief thing is to begin and to keep going, no matter the difficulties that may occur.

First of all there is the purely formal prayer, when we recite well-known prayers such as the Our Father and the Hail Mary. Then there is petitionary prayer in which we ask God for things or pray for other people. Thirdly there is everyday personal prayer. In this we either seek God's forgiveness for our failings or thank him for past and present gifts, such as life, love, the faith, our particular vocation, talents, gifts and so on and praise him for all he has done for us. These kinds of prayer are essentially basic but of themselves are not always sufficient. After all, what would our loved ones and friends think, let alone God, if we only addressed them either formally, when we wanted something from them, or in an abrupt or rudimentary way? What too would they say if we did all the talking and rarely allowed them a word? Even so, these methods of praying should not be despised. On the other hand, neither should they be confused with meditation, which is a form of thinking reflectively about the truths of our faith or the events in the life of Christ.

Then there is the Prayer of Quiet in which we try to create space in our lives, a state of affairs in which we are simply with God or trying to listen to him. In this kind of prayer we say nothing. Instead we are consumed with the wish to cultivate our awareness of God. It is the equivalent of being in the presence and company of someone we love – in silence and where words are unnecessary. This kind of silence is also a form of dialogue and this type of prayer is often attained by the use or utterance of a monosyllabic word such as peace, hope, joy, or love to sweep away as it were all thoughts, including good ones, in order to make space for God in our hearts and minds. However, even this level of prayer eventually becomes dissatisfying, like walking in the foothills when we could be climbing the higher mountains in the distance.

Before we can attain to a higher level of prayer, however, we have to leave all consolations and pleasure in prayer behind. We have to appreciate more than ever our need of God, and risk our prayer lives becoming dry and hard. If we persevere, up the rock face you might say, we then enter into pure prayer where the soul goes to God in prayer and, according to Thomas Merton, 'It reaches him without thoughts . . . Time no longer means anything in such prayer . . . For this prayer belongs less to time than to eternity' (*No Man Is An Island*).

Before we get to this stage, however, some of us become disheartened or even frightened, after all 'It is a fearful thing to fall into the hands of the living God.' Some are tempted to abandon prayer altogether, but to give in to such feelings is to kill prayer. The golden rule is to keep praying.

Finally, there is what Merton terms the purest prayer of all, which he says is not possible to reflect upon until it is over. He describes it as belonging to another order of things, as in some way debased by reflecting upon it, and as seeking to keep itself completely hidden in God. 'The experience,' he says, 'remains in our spirit like a wound, like a scar that will not heal . . .

This living wound may become a source of knowledge.'

A SENSE OF PEACE

Wherever we may have reached in prayer, however, and whatever way we may actually pray, the more we strive to make our prayer unselfish the more we shall experience a deep sense of peace. This is true especially when we attempt to keep God's commandments of love, for it is then that God makes his 'home' with us (John 14:23-4). God's presence with us then acts as the touchstone of all that we do and, in addition to peace, it enables us to discern whether or not we are genuinely loving him and being of service to others.

> 'Anybody who receives my commandments and keeps them will be one who loves me; and anybody who loves me will be loved by my Father, and I shall love him and show myself to him.' (John 14:21)

Furthermore, this sense of peace affects those to whom we relate. I discovered this a few years ago when a man in his sixties, who had been married for over forty years, collapsed while cutting the hedge in his garden. As he was falling to the ground with a massive heart attack, he shouted for his wife who came running to assist him. He died in her arms a few moments later uttering her name.

This man had been an invalid for most of his life. He had the use of only one leg and one lung and for that reason had been unable to obtain any health or life insurance. When the ambulance men arrived to take his body away, they found only a few pounds in his pockets. He had no bank account or savings.

His widow had no money of her own and was unable to afford the funeral. She was also suffering from a variety of serious illnesses and was now compelled to apply for what was known as supplementary benefit, especially to enable her to pay the rent, and for food and electricity. Two weeks after the death of her husband, however, she still had not received any financial assistance and she was literally penniless. Whereas this state of affairs made me very worried and even angry, she remained calm. What she possessed and I lacked was interior peace, a gift from Christ himself who, with God the Father, had clearly come and made his home with her. Even so, I thought something had to be done and I therefore went to the local branch of the Department of Health and Social Security on her behalf.

I sat there waiting my turn among the poor, the deprived, the mentally disturbed, the unwashed, the unshaven, the smelly and those the worse for drink; those in other words at the bottom of the social pile. The sight of a priest sitting in their midst caused much loud comment, some merriment and some abuse. For the first time in my life I felt grateful to a man who was drunk and who kept repeating loudly, 'It's the priest himself. God bless you, Father!' My instinct was simply to run, to get out of that depressing waiting-room, to jump in my car and drive away. It was only my concern for the widow that kept me there.

Eventually I got the widow her money and ran the gauntlet of those waiting their turn only by remembering her faith in God and how, throughout the trauma of her husband's death, she remained at peace. It is that kind of peace that is available only from God; a peace that is usually acquired in prayer and which is associated with listening to God, rather than bombarding him with our own preoccupations.

As the writer Karl Adam once said, 'Prayer is the meeting of the human personality with the divine, in a great silence where all else is hushed, for God is speaking.' Silent union with God was equally advocated by the hermit martyr Charles de Foucauld.

> Prayer is that state in which the soul looks wordlessly on God, solely occupied with contemplating him, telling him with looks that it loves him, while uttering no words, even in thought ... while everything is silent and asleep, while everything is drowned in darkness, I live at the feet of my God, pouring out my heart in love of him telling him I love him, while he tells me I shall never love him as much as he loves me, however great my love may be.
>
> (J.F. Six, *Spiritual Autobiography of Charles de Foucauld*)

Such prayer, however, is often attained only after years of perseverance, of regular dedication each day to prayer, and after one has overcome frequent temptations to abandon prayer altogether as a waste of time or with the idea that it might be better to do something seemingly more practical. This is to overlook the fact that time devoted to God is never wasted, quite apart from how it enables us to become more fully alive. Before we can attain to such prayer, however, it is necessary that we acquire detachment of the kind I was compelled to remember when a friend of mine died recently.

As a young man during the Second World War this friend of mine, Michael Hollings, had been an officer in the Guards and everywhere he went he carried a haversack on his back. In it were all his favourite possessions, such as the watch his mother had given him, the razor his father had presented to him before he went overseas, his favourite book of poems and so on.

One day the area where he and his men were based was hit by enemy mortar fire. He jumped into a trench to take cover and left his haversack outside the trench. The next minute it received a direct hit and all his most valued possessions were blown up, totally destroyed. At first he was completely shocked and says he felt devastated. Then this feeling was replaced by one of relief. He felt somehow profoundly liberated.

From then on my friend vowed never to be attached to anything material ever again. Never again to be owned as it were by his possessions. And from then on it was impossible ever to give him even a present. If one attempted to do so, he would immediately say, 'Thank you. I know just the person who will like that.' He never owned anything ever again.

After the war he became a priest and then began a life of amazing prayer, rising at five every morning to practise contemplation and using only one room for himself in the house allotted to him by the Church. All the other rooms he gave over to the use of homeless or sick people.

When he died not so long ago his parish church was not big enough to accommodate all those who wished to attend his funeral, so it took place in a cathedral. He was remembered as someone who put his whole life at the service of God and his neighbour; a way of life he had adopted through commitment to prayer and detachment from material concerns.

THREE

FORGIVENESS:
AN ASPECT OF LOVING

THE PLACE OF FORGIVENESS

Not long ago I was giving a lecture on AIDS to university students when into the lecture theatre came a latecomer, a young woman with a glorious smile. All through the lecture I was very aware of her, especially at question time when she asked the most perceptive and intelligent questions of all. After question time she asked if she could speak with me privately, so I invited her to my office, offered her a seat and asked how I could be of help.

The girl began by stating that she was HIV-positive. Having worked for several years in the field of AIDS

I was not shocked to hear this and asked her to continue. She then informed me that her husband had divorced her when he had heard she was infected. I began to murmur some words of sympathy when she added that she had also had an abortion in case her baby might have been carrying the virus. By now I was becoming disturbed, wondering what else she could possibly tell me. Then she stated that she was homesick and wanted desperately to return to her family, but that if they knew her condition they would disown her.

For the first time in four years I was stunned, not knowing what to say. Then inexplicably I got up and beckoned her towards me. She walked across the room and I gave her a huge hug and then literally sat her down again in her chair. I then watched tears start to fall silently down her cheeks. 'I think you should know,' she said, 'that you are the first person to touch me in two years.' That remark shook me as much as all the other facts she had told me about herself and I recalled something that I had first heard long ago about suffering.

All the evil ever done has been done to God, because it is misuse of his good gifts, a rejection of the purposes he set in motion from the beginning. The crucified Jesus is the only accurate picture of God the world has ever seen and the hands that hold us in existence are pierced with unimaginable nails. (Bishop John Baker)

I asked the young woman what enabled her to keep going and she replied that it was only the example of Christians who had suffered before her and who had forgiven those who had made them suffer. Not for the first time I then began asking myself how a Christian should behave towards those with AIDS and those who are HIV-positive. After this encounter I always suggested to my lecture audiences the following ten points:

1. Be ready to offer compassionate care towards all who are living with the HIV infection, living in the shadow of death.

2. Repudiate any condemnation, rejection or judgement of those infected, including the idea that their sickness is a judgement from God.

3. Stress the crucial need for education about AIDS in our society, especially in families, schools, universities, work places, leisure centres and church organisations.

4. Endeavour to be with and pray with the dying and the bereaved.

5. Give people with AIDS time and service, no matter how humble, such as offer to shop for them, garden, listen to them, allow them to express their feelings of anger, hurt, pain, rejection and so on.

6. Express solidarity with those with AIDS if and when they are used as scapegoats, treated as lepers or denied their human and social rights, e.g. when

they lose their jobs or accommodation, are refused mortgages or insurance.

7. Anticipate their fears and anxieties about pain, approaching death, infecting others, thoughts of suicide, guilt and shame.

8. Recognise the needs of the families and friends of those with AIDS. Be ready to offer them assistance in time of bereavement.

9. In our attitude, behaviour and speech indicate the belief that it is the quality of life rather than the quantity of life that counts.

10. Stress the fact that quality of life includes the assurance of eternal life.

One feature of the lives of Christians endeavouring to live fulfilled lives, which can never be over-emphasised, is the stress they place on the need to forgive those who cause us suffering. This is apparent in the case of Corrie Ten Boom, the woman whom many regard as a modern saint for the work she did during the Second World War on behalf of the Jewish community in Holland, for which she was ultimately arrested and sent to Ravensbruck concentration camp.

After the war Corrie travelled the world lecturing on her experiences and the importance of her Christian faith in the camp. Then one day in 1947, whilst speaking in a church in Munich on how God forgives us, no matter how grave our sins, she saw in the audience a balding heavy-set man, wearing a grey overcoat and holding a brown felt hat. The next moment she remembered how this same man looked in a blue uniform, with a cap bearing a skull and crossbones emblem. This man had been a guard in Ravensbruck.

After the lecture the man came up and congratulated Corrie on her talk. He told her he had become a Christian and how he knew God had forgiven him. He held out his hand and asked Corrie to forgive him. For her part she, who had talked so glibly about forgiveness, found herself as though paralysed. She then remembered the words of Jesus, 'If you don't forgive others their trespasses, neither will your Father in heaven forgive yours.' Then she silently prayed for Christ's help.

In her account Corrie says, 'And so woodenly, mechanically, I thrust my hand into the one stretched out to me. And as I did, an incredible thing took place. The current started in my shoulder, raced down my arm, sprang into our joined hands. And then this healing warmth seemed to flood my whole being . . . I had never known God's love so immensely as I did then.' It is hard to forgive when we have been badly hurt. Most of us instinctively feel like retaliating when we are verbally abused, let alone when we meet someone who has treated us as Corrie was treated by the guard in Ravensbruck.

Why do we find it so hard to forgive, and why should we forgive? I am not referring to those occasions we witness on television when, for example, parents of murdered or abused children say they'll never forgive the perpetrators of the crimes committed against their children; such statements are usually uttered following a harrowing trial. I am thinking about quarrels within families, strife about petty things between people who live under the same roof, arguments and disputes with work associates, bitterness between friends or people who once loved one another, but who now feel betrayed or rejected.

Someone once said that we each have three selves: the person we think we are, the person others think we are, and the person we really are. We often carry notions around in our heads and hearts which make us suspicious of others, instead of enabling us to seek the good in them. This is illustrated in the story of the two monks, one young and one old, walking through a forest.

On reaching a river the monks came across a beautiful girl stranded on the river bank, unable to get across. Without hesitation the old monk lifted the girl into his arms and carried her across. Miles and hours later the young monk confronted the old one. Recalling the incident with the girl, the young monk confessed his utter disillusionment with the old monk. 'How could you, a religious bound to the vow of chastity, be so casual and unguarded in your contact with such an attractive girl?' he asked. The old monk gently replied, 'Yes, but I left her there on the bank of the river. You are still carrying her with you.'

WHY WE SHOULD FORGIVE

Many years ago when still at school, I arrived home for the summer holidays and found what I considered to be a strange woman living at my home. My parents told me her Christian name but forbade me to ask any more questions about her. A few weeks later the woman left without saying goodbye. Only then did my parents inform me that the woman was a prostitute who had tried to give up her way of life in London. She had obtained employment at the holiday camp in our village, but, when the owner had discovered her former way of life, he had dismissed her immediately. The woman then had nowhere to go, none of the villagers offered her any help except my parents who took her in. My parents considered the villagers' refusal to help the woman more serious than the woman's past.

In the Gospel story of the woman taken in adultery, Jesus did not approve the woman's behaviour but neither did he condemn her. What he did do was to expose the hypocrisy of the scribes and Pharisees who had set a trap in which to catch him. If Jesus had disagreed with the stoning of the woman caught in adultery, he would have been disobeying the Law of Moses which required adulterers to be stoned to death. On the other hand, if he had agreed with the stoning, he would have been disobeying the law of the Romans. Jews were forbidden by the Romans to execute anyone. Jesus avoided the trap set for him by declaring that any of the woman's accusers who was without sin should cast the first stone. They all left, beginning with the eldest. Jesus also did not condemn the woman but simply told her to sin no more. This episode compels us to ask how we regard others when they sin.

Such a question was once faced by Dr Sheila Cassidy, when in 1975 she was imprisoned and tortured in Chile for having given medical treatment to a revolutionary in need. Shortly after being tortured she was transferred to a cell where she found a battered copy of the Bible. She opened it and the first thing she saw was a picture of a man prostrate under lightning, thunder and hail; a man with whom she was able to identify. Then she looked closer and discovered in the upper part of the picture a mighty hand, in other words the hand of God, and the text of Romans chapter 8, to the effect that 'Nothing can separate us from the love of Christ.'

Whereas at first the bottom half of the picture meant so much to Sheila Cassidy, gradually the top half became the more powerful. From praying 'Lord, let me out of here', she changed to 'Not my will but thine be done.' Sheila became filled with freedom and even kindness towards her oppressors and prayed with the other prisoners. She says that 'We knew that this freedom we had behind strong walls was not imagination: it was a quite tangible reality.' Such is the freedom enjoyed by those who seek to become fully alive; a freedom which enables us not only to forgive those who have hurt us in some way, but even to be reconciled with them.

Three years ago, as I was walking to the shops in the pouring rain wearing a clerical collar, I experienced something which I had never considered could ever happen to me. Towards me came two youths, whose faces I did not see because I was too intent on keeping my umbrella up in the rain. As they passed me, the one nearest to me turned his head and spat over me. When I let out a shout, they both turned around, sneered, shouted abuse and kept walking.

I felt furious and then suddenly terribly humiliated, somehow unclean and somehow not human. I lowered my umbrella so as to allow the rain to pour over my head and shoulders, in an attempt to wash away the spittle from my face and neck. I arrived at the shops completely soaked.

For a long time I was unable to think calmly about what had happened, but probably for the first time ever, I found myself able to understand just a little of what it means to be abused and humiliated. Since then, the story of Christ's passion has meant much more to me. What impressed me most after what occurred, was Christ's forgiveness of those who humiliated and abused him. Should we do less?

FOUR

CONVERSION:
A PRELIMINARY TO
LOVING

For many years, I have had a friend Paul – now in his mid sixties– the tenor of whose life is best described as one of searching. As a baby he was baptised, but his earliest recollections of religion are of attending Sunday school classes at the local branch of the Salvation Army. Indeed, until he was about seven, those religious manifestations which left the deepest mark on him were the sight of his mother kneeling by her bed every night to say her prayers, and the teaching he received on Jesus' parable of the Good Samaritan from the Salvation Army. At a very tender age then, the importance of both prayer and service of others was impressed upon him. He had little or no experience or knowledge of the Church and of the sacraments.

Then at the age of nine, without any prior warning or consultation, Paul was sent four hundred miles from home to a military boarding school. For the next nine years military discipline, martial law and customs formed the ethos in which he grew to manhood. He learnt how to drill, how to wear an army uniform correctly and how to handle a variety of weapons. Church parade on Sunday mornings and the school chaplain reading aloud excerpts from John Bunyan's *Pilgrim's Progress* on Sunday evenings are his chief recollections of organised religion. And yet he never forgot the memory of his mother at prayer or what the Salvationists had taught him about the paramount importance of caring for others. So strong were these recollections at times that he sometimes felt as though the harsh military atmosphere in which he lived was unreal; behind the everyday world of kit inspections, route marches and the study of regimental history was the real world of good triumphing over evil.

One day, not long after settling into the routine of military school life, the young boy was walking alone on the sands by the sea close to where the school was situated. Admittedly the setting was dramatic in the sense that before him stretched the open sea of the Atlantic and behind him high cliffs and seemingly endless miles of sand-dunes, but suddenly Paul became oblivious of everything around him; for a period of time (he has no means of knowing how long), he knew himself to be utterly in the presence of God himself. Furthermore, he knew deep within himself that he would always thereafter, if he so chose, be conscious of the presence of God wherever he happened to be. Today he remembers the occurrence as vividly as though it happened yesterday. From time to time, particularly in times of crisis and of seeking renewal, he pays a visit to the beach where as a boy he was converted to experiencing the presence of God.

At the time Paul found nothing strange about his conversion. He told no one about it, chiefly because it was precious to him. This incidentally tells us much about the natural way that children so often accept the supernatural, whereas later as adults they might find such things embarrassing. Paul simply incorporated the experience into his devotional life, now focusing his prayers on the person he had encountered on the beach and whom he identified as Christ. Apart from being regarded henceforth as a boy who took religion seriously, he was, outwardly at least, little different from his peers. It was gradually assumed by staff and pupils alike, as well as by Paul himself, that one day he would be a priest.

A DEEPER DISCOVERY

These comfortable assumptions were rudely shattered when Paul was seventeen. It was then that he first came across the monastic way of life. In the school holidays he started visiting monastic communities and studying their history. He was particularly attracted by the fact that the faith of these men living in community seemed to impinge on every aspect and every moment of their lives; theirs was not a religion confined to Sundays.

The commandant or headmaster of the military school and Paul's parents were bitterly hostile to this latest development. They interpreted it as a passing adolescent phase and did not for one moment suspect, since they knew nothing about earlier events, that it might be a further development of the youth's conversion on the beach eight years previously.

The parents' fears proved justified. After university and once he had turned twenty-one, their son expressed the wish to become a monk. Paul's parish priest nevertheless had the wisdom to persuade him to wait for at least two years, in order that he might test his vocation in the context of an ordinary community, in other words a parish. This period of testing proved invaluable in the sense that it enabled the young man to grow in his understanding of men and women as they really were, rather than in the abstract, and to determine how strong was his vocation to the monastic life. Under the guidance of his parish priest he also deepened his prayer life, began to appreciate the beauty of God's creation, the world around him, as well as begin to grasp his future responsibility as a monk to be concerned for all those in pain and need in the world. He grew therefore in his understanding that the detachment he would be required to have as a monk did not mean turning his back on the world and the human beings, made in God's image, who inhabited it; a world into which God had sent his only Son, out of love for his creation. The kind of detachment the young man began to cultivate was detachment from his own selfish tendencies, which then stood in the way of both his love of God and of his fellow human beings.

A SECOND CONVERSION

Later, when Paul had completed his novitiate at the monastery and just before he took first or simple vows, he experienced a second conversion which left as indelible an impression on him as the first. This time it was of the type mentioned in mystical theology by such reliable guides as Catherine of Siena, Teresa of Avila and John of the Cross. It was of the kind characterised by a passive purgation of the senses and a quickening of all one's insights into the realities lying behind human existence. He rarely speaks of the occasion, but, when pressed to do so, immediately disclaims any merit of his own for what occurred.

If he can be persuaded, Paul will describe how one day he was in the monastery grounds, sitting on a garden wall and gazing into the distance beyond a valley immediately below him. Without warning he experienced what seemed like a passage out of time. He also became acutely aware of being enveloped in an enormous silence which was quite the opposite of emptiness. Then he felt airborne and lifted up. He had the sensation of being high in the sky and circling round and round like an eagle with the earth beneath him. He was able to see both below and far into the distance all that was happening, but in slow motion so to speak. There seemed to be nothing that escaped his eye, from the usually unnoticed sway of each individual tree with its own particular shape and colour to the hum and buzz of all the tiny human beings moving to and fro in their cars and buses and on their bicycles. In himself he was both elated and utterly calm. He wanted this awareness to last forever. He also knew that what was being granted was a foretaste of eternity or what occurs at the resurrection of the body, without being able to put it adequately into words. It was an experience he was never to forget; the memory of it always gave him hope and a longing to experience it again.

THE NATURE OF LOVE

Much more important and simultaneous with this occurrence was the insight he was granted, at a level previously unknown to him, into what can only be termed the love motive in creation and which he later found described in the writings of Catherine of Siena.

Catherine maintains that on gazing into himself God fell in love with the beauty of his creatures-to-be and the creation of human beings was therefore an act of love. Not content with having love as the foundation of creation and creating human beings in his own image, God willed that human beings' ultimate purpose should be to inherit eternal life. Moreover, when this destiny was risked by humans' sinning, it was love again which accounted for the incarnation and which subsequently impelled Jesus to suffer the cross on their behalf and so redeem them. As St John writes:

> God's love for us was revealed when God sent into the world his only Son so that we could have life through him; this is the love I mean: not our love for God, but God's love for us when he sent his Son to be the sacrifice that takes our sins away. (1 John 4:9-10)

The nature of love, whether of God or of one's neighbour, is what teased the mind of Pope Clement I in his letter to the people of Corinth in which he wrote:

> Who can describe the constraining power of a love for God? Its majesty and its beauty who can adequately express? No tongue can tell the heights to which love can uplift us. Love binds us fast to God. Love casts a veil over sins innumerable. There are no limits to love's endurance, no

end to its patience. Love is without servility, as it is without arrogance. Love knows of no divisions, promotes no discord; all the works of love are done in perfect fellowship. It was in love that all God's chosen saints were made perfect; for without love nothing is pleasing to him. It was in love that the Lord drew us to himself . . . Its perfection is beyond all words.

It necessarily follows therefore, as St John succinctly pointed out, that anyone who says he loves God and hates his brother is a liar, 'since a man who does not love his brother that he can see cannot love God, whom he has never seen' (1 John 4:20). Love indeed is at the root of the concern we should all have for our fellow men and women, especially the poor and dispossessed, who comprise the community of human-kind and who are made in God's image.

This was just one insight, but the most important one, which was granted to Paul. Occasionally thereafter he encountered people who had had similar experiences. Those who genuinely had been granted a glimpse of eternity, as distinct from those who simply possessed lively imaginations, could usually be discerned by their grave difficulty in describing it adequately, and by their treasuring it as something precious and as marking a milestone in their lives. More often than not, they also disarmed the sceptical by their smiling conviction that there was nothing that made them more 'special' than other people. It was not so much the experience as the insight granted them that mattered, and which they considered to be beyond price. This idea is reflected in a poem by Richard Spender, who was killed during the Second World War.

Is this sorrow, God, this sickness
The price we must pay?
Is this unbounded emptiness, O God, this heart
   wringing,
The sum that we must render
For that one, dear, treasured glimpse
Of High Eternity?
Yes God!
For that swift flight beyond the earth-bound clouds
Would I again pay tears and weariness,
For one bright flash of Heaven-born flame
Would I again fall burnt and torn to earth.
That soaring through the rack and grey-scarred
   night
Was worth the unrelaxing frown of tight-lipped
Death.
But God, of Thy mercy, grant, Everlasting
More star-fired sight, more flame, O lofty One,
   more light!
     (Richard Spender in *The Wisdom of the English
               Mystics,* ed. Robert Way)

The sadness, as well as the ineffable joy, hinted at by Spender is also experienced by Paul in the monastery, but in his case it is occasioned by the fact that he is aware that he lacked the courage to persist on the journey; he knows that after a second conversion a third is necessary. But before that can occur one is usually required to undergo 'the dark night of the soul'. From that my friend shied and continues to shy away.

Paul, who long ago as a solitary child experienced conversion on an Atlantic beach and encountered the person of Christ, has now been a monk for over thirty years. His commitment to Christ is now unthinkable outside a community context, a fact which throws even further light on this whole question of achieving real happiness in the service of others.

FIVE

COMMUNITY:
A DIMENSION OF LOVING

VALYERMO: A MONASTIC COMMUNITY

Just over an hour's journey by car from Los Angeles and beyond the San Gabriel Mountains to the east of the city, there lies the Mojave Desert. Most of it is a hot and forbidding plateau, splattered with oddly shaped hills or pockmarked with steep gorges, dried-up valleys and massive rock formations. The vegetation consists largely of cactus plants, curious-looking Joshua trees and brown scrub. The wild life includes rabbits, squirrels, snakes, lizards, spiders and racoons. The only view travellers generally have of this desert is from a plane en route either to or from Las Vegas, that artificial city built in the desert solely for gambling and entertainment.

Precisely because the desert is so unattractive to the traveller and tourist with their cameras and their prying eyes, it is ideal for the location of military establishments. It is here therefore that one finds both air force and army bases and the fairly frequent sound of planes flying low. Slightly further to the east and into Nevada lie the even more ominous nuclear testing grounds.

At the heart of all this super-power weaponry and sabre rattling, however, there is something one hardly expects: a green and fertile oasis. What makes this particular oasis so special, with its trees, flowers and plants, its interesting bird and animal life, as well as its springs, streams and lake, is the fact that it lies within the grounds of a Benedictine monastery. This is the last thing one would expect to come across in the Mojave Desert and as a neighbour to military establishments. Its name is Valyermo.

Once upon a time it was a cattle ranch and many of its buildings still retain the atmosphere of such a place – simple one-storey buildings and white painted fences marking the edge of the property. As one approaches along a drive, the first sign one comes across reads 'No hunting, except for Peace'.

It seems ironic as well as oddly fitting that a place of prayer, beauty and quiet should be situated in the middle of noise and military bases and close to nuclear testing sites. In one place we have, as it were, the symbols of the completely opposing choices facing the human race. I have heard it argued too that it is the prayer and fasting, the asceticism and intercessions of the monks, rather than the military weapons that are keeping America secure. A visit to Valyermo enables one to echo the words of Thomas Merton about his own monastery, Gethsemane in Kentucky:

> This is the centre of all the hidden vitality that is in America. These men, hidden in the anonymity of their choir ... are doing for their land what no army, no congress, no president could ever do as such: they are winning for it the grace and the protection and the friendship of God.
>
> (*Elected Silence*)

Valyermo is remarkable in many ways. In the early 1930s a handful of Belgian monks set out from Europe to establish a Benedictine monastery in China. They quickly made friends, opened a school and dispensary, preached the gospel and had the joy of seeing several young Chinese join them as novices. This monastery lasted until the Communist takeover of China in 1949, when the monks were humiliated, put on an obviously rigged public trial, ostensibly for carrying out imperialist and subversive activities, and then imprisoned. In 1950 the European monks were expelled from China, travelled to California, bought the land of Valyermo and started afresh. Two Chinese monks remained behind. Eventually one of them died, whilst the other was held in prison for the next twenty-six years, often in solitary confinement and shackled by his wrist to the wall of his prison cell. His name was Brother Peter.

Brother Peter retained his sanity by reciting the Psalms and by praying. He consistently refused to deny his membership of the Church, his Christian faith and especially his belief that Jesus was the Son of God. Finally, when China once again opened its doors to the outside world, Brother Peter was found to be one of the more fortunate of imprisoned Chinese Christians, having survived torture and long years of captivity. In 1982 he was released and he was able to rejoin his fellow monks, now rehoused in the United States at Valyermo.

When I first saw Brother Peter in the chapel at Valyermo, I was led to reflect on Thomas Merton's definition of a monk and gradually I began to understand, at least to a certain extent, the reason for Brother Peter's survival.

> The monk is a man of sorrow, a man discontented with every illusion, aware of his own poverty, impatient of evasion, who seeks the naked realities that only the desert can reveal. But the monk is also a man of joy, a man at peace with the emptiness of the wilderness, glad of his limitations, loving reality as he finds it, and therefore secure in his humility. He is a man of joy and a man of sorrow both together because he is a man of desires. And because he lives by pure hope, he

has entered into the secret which Christ has taught His chosen ones: that hope gives us, even on earth, the secure possession of our inestimable heritage as sons of God. What is this inheritance, and what is this possession? It is the wisdom by which we find God in the Mystery of His Christ. It is the wisdom given by His Spirit to those who have left all things to follow Him – the wisdom of the Cross.

(Silence in Heaven)

Using this insight as my starting point and because I wanted to study the monks' way of life at Valyermo at first hand, I subsequently requested permission to live and work alongside them; not to be treated as a guest, but as a member of the community following their daily routine in every respect. For the next few weeks therefore I rose at 5 o'clock every morning and followed a routine of prayer, study and work until 9 o'clock at night, when I usually fell into bed exhausted. Prayer entailed singing the psalms and prayers of the Office in church several times a day, participating in daily Community Mass and spending time in personal prayer. Study involved spiritual reading twice a day, attending classes given by the Novice Master on the history of monasticism or the writings of one of the Fathers of the early Church, and twice a week receiving talks from the Abbot. Work meant setting meal tables for guests and monks in the refectory, washing mountains of dishes three times a day, cleaning cells and bathrooms, working in the monastery business office, making beds and preparing rooms for visitors.

From this unchanging and often relentless routine I obtained a greater understanding of two things. The first was Benedictine peace, which is not at all a matter of being disengaged from life, but much more a protest against our frequent adjustment and accommodation to worldly values in our society. And the second thing I came to understand more fully was the meaning and purpose of community. For the first time I began to comprehend why a Christian cannot obtain real happiness or personal fulfilment outside the context of a community, whether the community be a parish, a monastery or convent, or even a family or gathering of like-minded individuals. A sense of community often follows hard on the heels of a conversion to Christ. Without it a Christian's faith remains undeveloped and concepts of fellowship remain untried.

THE MEANING OF COMMUNITY

In his deeply moving book *Community and Growth*, which was first put into my hands by the Abbot of Valyermo, Jean Vanier teaches us a great deal about the strengths and weaknesses of community living. If we are lonely and unhappy, community can be a place of sharing; on the other hand, it can also be the occasion for discovering our frustrations, selfishness and limitations. In other words, community is usually a revelatory experience.

Vanier points out that we in the West have much to learn about community from the people of Africa and India who often live it rather than discuss it. He tells of the aborigines of Australia who buy nothing except cars, in order to visit their clan, since the link of brotherhood is what they value most. He describes Mother Teresa saying, 'My people are hungry.' And he goes on to say:

> "My people" are my community, which is both the small community, those who live together, and the larger community which surrounds it and for which it is there. "My people" are those who are written in my flesh as I am in theirs. Whether we are near each other or far away, my brothers and sisters remain written within me. I carry them, and they, me; we know each other again when we meet. To call them "my people" doesn't mean that I feel superior to them, or that I am their shepherd or that I look after them. It means that they are mine as I am theirs. There is a solidarity between us. What touches them, touches me. And when I say "my people" I don't imply that there are others I reject. My people is my community made up of those who know me and carry me. They are the springboard towards all humanity. I cannot be a universal brother, unless I first love my people.

In certain parishes it is extremely hard to foster a sense of community, especially when people do not live and work in the same area, schools are no longer neighbourhood establishments, and commuting even for worship has become the norm.

In the past thirty years or so there has been a phenomenal increase in the number and variety of Christian lay communities throughout the world. In Britain these range, for example, from charismatically-orientated groups, to communities with distinct charisms and aims, such as the Upper Room Community in St Alban's, the Prince of Peace Community in Baldock in Hertfordshire, the New Creation Community in Liverpool which concentrates on retreat work, the Jesuit Volunteer Community in Manchester largely concerned with social justice issues, and the Worth Abbey Lay Community.

When lay communities have been established, however, it is often necessary for their members to take to heart two fundamentally important lessons touched on by Jean Vanier. The first is that there is no such thing as a perfect community: the personal equilibrium and harmony that people dream of, usually come about only after considerable struggle and then only intermittently. The second lesson is that if any community forgets service to others, it will fail.

A community gradually discovers as it grows that it is not there simply for itself. It belongs to humanity. It has received a gift which must bear fruit for all people. If it closes in on itself, it will suffocate ... A community must always remember that it is a sign and witness for all mankind. Its members must be faithful to each other if they are to grow. But they must also be faithful as a sign and source of hope for all mankind.

(Community and Growth)

It is interesting to compare Vanier's words with those of Bruno Bettelheim writing of his experience of the kibbutz movement.

Communal life can flourish only if it exists for an aim outside itself. Community is viable if it is the outgrowth of a deep involvement in a purpose which is other than, or above, that of being a community.

(Home for the Heart)

This is especially true in a world where there is real hunger for food, human rights, medical facilities, decent housing, education, and relief from natural disasters, political oppressors and violence.

While no community should exist solely for itself, neither should it overlook what it might learn and receive from those it seeks to serve. Vanier is adamant that, ultimately, the most important lesson to be learnt by any community is that it should not do things for the needy, but should rather assist the needy to grow in confidence in themselves and discover their own gifts. That is real service.

The late Dominic Gaisford, Abbot of Worth Abbey, once described his vision of a monastery in today's world. In doing so he also gave a description of the role and purpose of all Christian communities, worthy of the name monastic or lay.

> Monasteries should be warm and open places where friendship and affection can be given without fear, where we seek the best in people without abrasive competition, where efficiency is tempered by solicitude, where all the complexities of sin in us are slowly healed in prayer and the sacraments, and where hope is found. It is not easy to integrate all the conflicting elements in us, ranging from sexuality via fruitful work and intellectual satisfaction to the search for God in himself and in others, but it can and must be done if we monks are to fulfil our vocation as prophets and witnesses to the Good News of Jesus Christ.
> (*A Touch of God*)

SIX

COMPASSION:
AN INGREDIENT OF LOVING

WHAT IS COMPASSION?

In his autobiography the Russian poet Yevtushenko describes an incident in Moscow during 1941. The streets of the city were lined with people, chiefly women, waiting for a parade of German prisoners of war to pass by. A feeling of hatred was tangible in the crowd for nearly every woman present had lost a husband, father, brother or son to the German invaders and this was their opportunity to express their loathing. Then the German prisoners came into view:

Thin, unshaven, wearing dirty blood-stained bandages, hobbling on crutches or leaning on the shoulders of their comrades . . . the streets became dead silent. An old woman pushed through the crowd, past the police cordon and, taking something from her coat, pushed it into the pocket of an exhausted soldier – a crust of black bread. And now suddenly from every side women were running towards the soldiers, pushing into their hands bread, cigarettes, whatever they had. The soldiers were no longer enemies. They were people.

In their book *Compassion*, Henri Nouwen, Donald McNeill and Douglas Morrison tell us:

Compassion asks us to go where it hurts, to enter into places of pain, to share in brokenness, fear, confusion, and anguish. Compassion challenges us to cry out with those in misery, to mourn with those who are lonely, to weep with those in tears. Compassion requires us to be weak with the weak, vulnerable with the vulnerable, and powerless with the powerless. Compassion means full immersion in the condition of being human.

JESUS AND COMPASSION

These same authors go on to show how Jesus in his life on earth gave abundant evidence of being compassionate. When he saw the crowds harassed and dejected like sheep without a shepherd, he was deeply touched (Matthew 9:36). When confronted with the blind, the paralysed and the deaf, he shared their pain (Matthew 14:14). When faced with four thousand hungry and tired people, he was moved (Mark 8:2). He responded in a similar way when he came across the widow of Nain about to bury her only son (Luke 7:13), a leper who fell at his knees (Mark 1:41), and the two blind men who called after him (Matthew 9:27).

The authors of *Compassion* go to the very heart of why Jesus was compassionate and why we too should behave similarly towards others in need. They discuss at length the concept of *kenosis* or self-emptying which Jesus underwent on behalf of the human race. This *kenosis* is concerned with how Jesus became not only fully human, but took on himself the role of a servant and ultimately died on the cross, in order to rescue us from our slavery to sin. In other words, in his incarnation, Jesus, though remaining fully divine, deliberately chose not to occupy a position of power and majesty. He became like us in all things except sin; in the words of the deeply moving early Christian hymn:

> His state was divine,
> yet he did not cling
> to his equality with God
> but emptied himself

to assume the condition of a slave,
and became as we are;
and being as we are,
he was humbler yet,
even to accepting death,
death on a cross.

(Philippians 2:6-8)

If Jesus behaved compassionately, can Christians do less? Jesus gave the example of service to his disciples at the Last Supper when he washed their feet. He also describes what will occur when he returns to earth at the end of time; when those who fed the hungry, gave drink to the thirsty, welcomed strangers, clothed the naked and visited those who were sick or in prison will inherit the kingdom prepared for them, whereas those who neglected to be compassionate will be punished (Matthew 25:31-46).

Our compassion must extend towards and embrace the poorest of the poor, the kind of people for whom Mother Teresa of Calcutta deliberately opened her homes.

My house is that
– of those one tries to avoid for fear of contagion and dirtiness, because they are covered with microbes and worms;
– of those who do not go out to pray, because one cannot go out of one's house naked;

– of those who do not eat any more, because they have no strength for eating;
– of those who fall down in the streets knowing that they are going to die, and at whose side pedestrians pass and don't look back;
– of those who do not weep any more, because they have run out of tears;
– of the untouchable.

(Mother Teresa in *Heart of Joy*,
Servant Publications, 1987)

AN EXAMPLE OF COMPASSION

Compassion is not of course the preserve of those who consider themselves healthy. One of the most compassionate people it was my privilege to meet was a boy of fifteen called Jamie, who was intelligent, athletic, and popular with his school friends. Then, without warning, Jamie was struck down with cancer of the spine.

For the next twelve to eighteen months, Jamie was obliged to accept not only the gradual decline of his ability to move, but the advancing spectre of death. Despite this and despite increasing pain, he never once complained. There were obviously occasions when he felt depressed and became a prey to doubts and fears, but such occasions were rare.

Jamie's suffering affected not just his family, his school associates, and fellow Catholics in his home parish, but the whole village community in which he lived. Everyone who visited and spoke to Jamie came away feeling somehow uplifted and more caring; Jamie's inner strength and serenity increased as he approached closer to death. Even more impressive was the fact that his interest in and love for those around his sick bed grew. He clearly preferred to hear of the pain of others and to empathise with them, rather than to receive their sympathy. Jamie was supposed to be the sick one and yet it was Jamie who was, in a sense, healing others with his compassion. His conduct reflected the sort of love described by the late Henri Nouwen in his book *Intimacy*.

> Love is not based on the willingness to listen, to understand the problems of others, or to tolerate their otherness. Love is based on the mutuality of the confession of our total self to each other. This makes us free to declare not only: "My strength is your strength" but also: "Your pain is my pain, your weakness is my weakness, your sin is my sin." It is from this intimate fellowship of the weak that love is born.

At Jamie's funeral there was standing room only, a testimony to the extent to which his courage and victorious struggle had affected so many. It was also a remarkably joyous occasion. While the keynote of the ceremony was relief that Jamie's sufferings were now at an end, there was also a sense in which we all felt indebted to him for having taught us through his suffering and 'other-centredness' that compassion is an integral part of the service of others. With Jamie's death I began to understand the words of Metropolitan Anthony:

> With every person who dies, part of us is already in eternity. We must, if we love this person, live up to the great encounter of a living soul with a living God. We must let go of everything that was small, that was separation, alienation and estrangement, and reach out to that serenity and greatness, newness and abundance of life into which the departed person has entered ... We should not speak of our love in the past tense. Love is a thing that does not fade in a faithful heart. It does not go into the past unless we betray our love ... Our love cannot be dead because a person has died. If that is true, our life must be a continuation of theirs, with all its significance. We must reflect on all that was beauty, and nobility, in that person, and make sure those around us, and our surroundings, do not lose anything through death.

CONCERN FOR THOSE WHO SUFFER

Faced with suffering, should we speak out or remain silent? Elie Wiesel, a survivor of the Holocaust, was of the view that, 'If someone suffers and he keeps silent, it can be a good silence. If someone suffers and I keep silent, then it is a destructive silence.' As he said in his acceptance speech when awarded the Nobel Peace Prize:

> I swore never to be silent whenever and wherever human beings endure suffering humiliation. We must always take sides. Neutrality helps the oppressor, never the victim. Silence encourages the tormentor, never the tormented. Sometimes we must interfere. When human lives are endangered, when human dignity is in jeopardy, national borders and sensitivities become irrelevant. Whenever men and women are persecuted because of their race, religion or political view, that place must – at that moment – become the centre of the universe.

If we fail to be concerned for such people, to pray for them and to work for the alleviation of their misery, we shall be failing to hear Christ's words, 'I tell you solemnly, in so far as you neglected to do this to one of the least of these, you neglected to do it to me' (Matthew 25:46).

According to the World Bank 40 per cent of people in the Third World are living in absolute poverty; they do not possess anywhere near adequate daily food, housing or clothing. In tropical and subtropical countries more than 14 million children under the age of four die each year of starvation. In India 70 per cent of its total waters are polluted. According to the World

Health Organisation in the next decade millions of men and women will die of AIDS in Africa alone. Moreover the majority of world surveys suggest that, if present trends continue, the world will become more crowded, more polluted, less ecologically stable and more vulnerable to political and economic disruption than ever previously. Under these circumstances a Christian cannot attain total fulfilment or even achieve real happiness by standing idly by.

SEVEN

SAINTS:
ICONS OF LOVING

AN ENCOUNTER

A few years ago I was invited to supper by a woman whose passion is to bring together people of similar interests. Around the table that evening were politicians, businessmen, military people and diplomats. As a priest, I wondered what I had in common with such people but, knowing my hostess, I knew there had to be something.

Next to me my hostess had placed an Italian woman of about my own age who lives in Rome. For a short while I thought that must be what we had in common: a love of Rome. But that seemed to me a somewhat inadequate reason. She might just as well have placed me next to someone from New York, another city I love.

At first the conversation between the Italian woman and myself was somewhat desultory. Then, for some obscure reason, we began talking about saints and saints are my passion. The woman giving the supper party was well aware that I devour books on the saints; I used to collect relics of them; I still visit their shrines, I invoke them at every turn and I think of them as one thinks of close friends.

It is not difficult therefore to understand the excitement I felt when my neighbour informed me that she was the niece of Blessed Pier Giorgio Frassati. Pier Giorgio Frassati was born in 1901, the son of the founder and editor of the Italian newspaper *La Stampa*. He was a student at Turin University, a skier, a mountaineer, an athlete, the possessor of a wonderful sense of humour and a deeply convinced Christian. During his short life he devoted his spare time to working among the poor in the slums of Turin, to nursing the sick and to raising the consciousness of his fellow students about the faith. Pier Giorgio died aged twenty-four of polio, which he contracted nursing the sick. Hundreds of the poorest of Turin flocked to his funeral. After his death a cult began, people sought his intercession and miracles occurred. He was beatified in 1990 by Pope John Paul II who referred to him as the Man of the Beatitudes. It was

wonderful to meet his niece and I was deeply grateful
to my hostess for making this possible.

Why should anyone be fascinated by the saints?
Perhaps because during their lives on earth they were
the most alive of their contemporaries. The created
universe is a theatre of God's activity and what occurs
in it is a rehearsal for the even richer life of the world
to come. The saints knew this.

THE VARIETY AMONG SAINTS

No two saints are the same. One has only to think
of the differences between Benedict, Thomas Becket,
Clare, Philip Neri or Bernadette. Their concern for
others often took on staggering proportions as with
Maximilian Kolbe who voluntarily took the place of
a condemned prisoner in Auschwitz, or Father Damian
who worked among lepers, dressing their wounds,
building their houses and digging their graves, until
he became a leper himself.

Above all, because saints are fully alive, they demonstrate an amazing capacity for love of God. This is
particularly so in the case of Augustine writing in
Book X of his *Confessions*. Augustine asks of God:

> What do I love when I love Thee? Not beauty of
> bodies, nor the fair harmony of time, not the
> brightness of the light, so lovely to the eye, not
> the soft melodies of many songs, nor the sweet

smell of flowers and ointments and spices, nor manna and honey, nor the limbs acceptable to embraces by the flesh. None of these I love when I love my God. Yet I love a kind of light and melody and fragrance and meat and embracement, when I love my God, and these are . . . of my inner man: where there shineth unto my soul what space cannot contain, and there soundeth what time beareth not away, and there smelleth what breathing disperseth not . . . This is what I love when I love my God.

SAINTS PETER AND PAUL

One of the earliest of Christian beliefs is that of the communion of saints, the doctrine that from their place in heaven the saints are not forgetful of those of us still struggling on earth and that they are ever ready to intercede for us. This was believed to be particularly so in the case of martyrs whose witness was considered perfect and who were thought to have been 'reborn' into everlasting life at the moment of their death.

Such saints as Peter and Paul are able to repay our study of them, if only because they continue even today to serve as examples of Christian living. According to the second-century apocryphal documents the Acts of Paul and Thecla, St Paul was short, bald, bow-legged, possessing a grizzled beard, knitted eyebrows, a long nose, stooping shoulders, looking one moment like a man and the next like an angel. And although not in the least handsome, Paul was also what we would call a colossus. Erasmus talked of him as 'thundering and lightening and talking sheer flame'. Luther adored him and spoke of him as a 'poor tough little mannikin'. A modern writer, Robert Payne, says that 'Paul lived in visions, forever blinded by the vision of Damascus.'

Of Peter's appearance we know little. We can only surmise from our knowledge of him as a Galilean fisherman that he was probably physically strong. On the other hand, there is plenty of evidence that his character and behaviour were an explosive mixture of elements, ranging from the impetuous and passionate to the downright cowardly. Peter's impulsive nature was to the fore when Jesus was seen walking on the water and Peter jumped out of his boat and, with great faith, walked towards him. But just as quickly, he began to doubt, and sank beneath the waves. At the Last Supper Peter initially refused to have his feet washed and then wanted to be washed all over! When Jesus was arrested in Gethsemane, it was Peter who chopped off the ear of the high priest's servant. When Jesus was taken to the high priest's house, Peter denied knowing him three times. And yet it was this same Peter that Jesus was to confirm as leader of the apostles after the resurrection.

Paul, the intellectual and the Pharisee, enters history as the persecutor of the Christians. It was at his feet that those who stoned Stephen laid their clothes. But after his encounter with Christ on the road to Damascus, Paul eventually became the greatest missionary of all time. He also knew the meaning of suffering for his Lord and later claimed he had served Christ with

> ... far greater labours, far more imprisonments, with countless beatings and often near death. Five times I have received at the hands of the Jews the forty lashes less one. Three times I have been beaten with rods; once I was stoned. Three times I have been shipwrecked; a night and a day I have been adrift at sea; on frequent journeys, in danger from rivers, danger from robbers, danger from my own people, danger from Gentiles, danger in the city, danger in the wilderness, danger from false brethren; in toil and hardship, through many a sleepless night, in hunger and thirst, often without food, in cold and exposure. (2 Corinthians 11:23-7)

And yet Paul persevered and still at the heart of the message he preached was love.

> Though I speak with the tongues of men
> and angels,
> And have not love
> I am become as sounding brass
> Or a tinkling cymbal.
>
> (1 Corinthians 13:1)

Peter loved no less, but his love took the form of leadership. He spoke at Pentecost, was freed by an angel from prison, was the first apostle to perform a miracle, spoke before the Sanhedrin and he dared to receive the Gentile Cornelius into the Church. For Paul, Peter was the first named witness to the Risen Christ (1 Corinthians 15:5), the source of Tradition about Christ (Galatians 1:18), the leader in Jerusalem at the time of Paul's first visit as a Christian, and an apostle to the circumcised as Paul was to the uncircumcised.

Whatever their differences (on one occasion Peter was rebuked to his face by Paul for giving in to the demands of Jewish Christians), Peter and Paul had at least three things in common: their readiness to confess that they were weak sinful men, their readiness to die as martyrs and the fact that they were both consumed by their relationship with Christ. As Paul was to say,

Who shall separate us from the love of Christ?
Shall tribulation or distress or persecution?
Or famine or nakedness? Or peril or sword?

(Romans 8:35)

Small wonder Peter and Paul remain an inspiration today for those suffering for their beliefs, those giving their lives in the service of others, those deprived of human rights, those enduring poverty, and those in sickness and pain. They are also, like all the saints, an inspiration for those Christians seeking to live totally fulfilled lives through a personal response to a call from God, a response not just of the mind, but of the heart, a response illustrated in their attitude and behaviour to other people.

WELCOME

The dynamics of welcome show whether or not we are serious and genuine. So often people knock as it were at our door and we make a gesture of hearing them, but in so many other ways we make it clear we are supposedly busy. In other words, the doors of our room are open but the door of our heart is closed. We fail to realise that to welcome the stranger is not just something mechanical but an attitude of mind and heart. It is also continuous and should never cease. It requires listening to other people, discerning within what they are endeavouring to say, engaging them in real dialogue which may even involve saying 'No' in a compassionate way. For all these reasons the first gestures of welcome are often the most important; they may cause people to flee or stay. We must always make the stranger feel that he or she has our whole attention, that they are important to us, that they are of value and that we care for them. This is particularly so with those who are vulnerable, those who are on the margins of society, those in need of hope, the inarticulate and the wounded. By our welcome, the stranger must be made to feel part of the community, in other words no longer a stranger but be made to feel at home.

St John begged his followers to ensure that their love for others should not consist of 'just words or mere talk, but something real and active' (1 John 3:18). He also insisted that 'Anyone who says "I love God" but hates his brother, is a liar, since a man who does not love the brother that he can see cannot love God, whom he has never seen' (1 John 4:20).

Love itself, which consumes both the saints and all true followers of Christ, has probably never been more famously or beautifully described than by St Paul in his first letter to the people of Corinth (1 Corinthians 13). However, as St Paul well knew and as a perceptive spiritual writer, the late John Dalrymple, observed, sooner or later love involves taking up one's cross.

> We human beings cannot love each other without going through experiences which tear us apart but mature us, experiences like conquering mistrust; learning to forgive the apparently unforgivable; exposing the private sectors of our being by letting the defences of human pride be broken down; learning to be patient and to conquer anger; having to apologize for humiliating faults; sharing what we thought was not for sharing; surrendering our independence in the higher interests of love.
>
> (*Costing Not Less Than Everything*)

The imperative to love both God and our neighbour

remains. Without attempting to fulfil it we remain only half alive, our full potential as human beings made in the image of God remains unrealised, and we cannot be truly happy. Our salvation indeed depends on it.

Some Fathers of the Church considered that the divine image in humans was found in their command over the rest of creation. Others preferred to believe that the divine image was located in the orientation of a person's spirit towards union with God. The Fathers also tended to distinguish between image and likeness. Some argued that the image is in our nature and the likeness is imparted by grace; others separated image into two kinds, that which humans possessed in the beginning and that which comes into being as a gift of the Holy Spirit. Even so, what matters is the command to love, a view shared by Clement of Alexandria who maintained that 'the true image of God is the man who does good' (*Stromata*, 2:19), and by Origen who remarked that, 'If you are merciful, the image of God is in you' (*Homilia in Leviticum*, 4:3). This is as true today as ever it was. In the words of Thomas Merton:

> To say that I am made in the image of God is to say that love is the reason for my existence; for God is love. Love is my true identity. Selflessness is my true self. Love is my true characteristic. Love is my name. I who am without love cannot become love unless Love identifies me with

himself. But if he sends his own love, himself, to act and love in me and in all that I do, then I shall be transformed, I shall discover who I am and shall possess my true identity by losing myself in him. And that is what is called sanctity.

(*Seeds of Contemplation*)

EIGHT

MARRIAGE:
AN IMAGE OF LOVING

AN OBSERVATION

Not long ago I was invited by a colleague to visit his parish and give a talk on marriage. A few days later he rang me to say he was worried because some of his parishioners had complained that 'a single, male, celibate priest would know nothing about marriage.' He wanted to know what I thought about this. I told him I was still prepared to visit his parish if that's what he wanted.

When I arrived there I found awaiting me an audience of about one hundred people, young and old, of both sexes and apparently interested to hear what

I had to say. Before beginning the talk I had prepared on the subject, I quietly announced that there were one or two things I wished to say by way of introducing myself.

I first announced that I was the product of a marriage and that for twenty years I had keenly observed the kind of relationship my parents had with each other. Because my father had been gassed and had been a prisoner in the First World War, he had been an invalid for the rest of his life, so I knew at close hand what it was like to experience debilitating sickness and pain in a marriage. Then, in the slump years of the 1930s my father had been made redundant, so I was able to observe what it meant for a married man, with a wife and two children to support, to be unemployed. One of the things it meant was that his family, including me, knew what it was to be poor. Another consequence was that my mother then had to go out to work, so I was able to see how this affected their marriage and their attitude towards each other. Then my brother was killed in the Second World War and I witnessed loss and bereavement within a marriage. Later my mother was involved in a serious car crash and badly injured, so I observed the effects of trauma on a marriage. Finally, at my father's death and through close observation of my mother, I understood the meaning of widowhood. I then asked the audience if any of them still considered I might be utterly ignorant about marriage.

A SACRAMENT

In virtually all Christian documents and statements concerning marriage and the family, we are told that these constitute the first and basic community of life and love. Ideally, it is in the family that the love of God is first experienced and the gospel first learned. The love of wife and husband is then conceived as a sharing in the life and love of God. Together, wife and husband explore the meaning of love and their experience of love is their way of discovering God's love for them.

Marriage is also often spoken of as an image of the union between Christ and his Church and in this context the family is sometimes referred to as the 'domestic church'. To describe this mystery and miracle of love the Church uses the word 'sacrament', and we need to recognise that for many people married life is their means of discovering God and their way to salvation, fulfilment, happiness and holiness. Gone are the days when holiness was thought of as primarily the prerogative of those in the ordained ministry or religious life.

This view of marriage and the family appeals to both the highest ideals of our faith and to our loftiest experiences of love.

It has been said that "To love another person is to see the face of God." And that is a perfect summary of the Christian theology of marriage. For such a vision of marriage enables the impossible to become possible; two people, drawn together by human love, are invited to transform that love into a sharing in the creative love of God and in so doing transform themselves and their partner into being more fully alive, to become the unique persons God created them to be.

(*Being Together*, CMO Publications)

Even so, the Christian has always been fully aware that human relationships in general and especially those of marriage do not develop and grow, let alone prosper, unless each partner is prepared to make endless efforts in the interest of willing the good of the other. Without this it is impossible for anyone and particularly married couples to experience the kind of love eloquently described by St Paul to the people of Corinth:

Love is always patient and kind; it is never jealous; love is never boastful or conceited; it is never rude or selfish; it does not take offence, and is not resentful. Love takes no pleasure in other people's sins but delights in the truth; it is always ready to excuse, to trust, to hope, and to endure whatever comes. (1 Corinthians 13:4–7)

MARRIAGE TODAY

The realisation that love within marriage and the family will only flourish through tremendous effort on the part of both husband and wife has never been more necessary than within the complex context of present-day society. The image of marriage and family as rock-like, permanent and durable, with man the breadwinner, woman the keeper of hearth and home, and children secure within the family disappeared long ago. Instead couples now have a quite different and more complex set of expectations, especially in terms of what they sometimes seek from each other. Nevertheless, when these expectations are fulfilled, the result is much more satisfying. This was shown in the relationship that C.S. Lewis enjoyed with his wife.

> A good wife contains so many persons in herself. What was H. not to me? She was my daughter, my mother, my pupil, my teacher, my subject and my sovereign; and always holding all these in solution, my trusty comrade, friend, shipmate, fellow soldier. My mistress: but at the same time all that any man friend (and I have good ones) has ever been to me. Perhaps more.
>
> (*A Grief Observed*,
> Faber and Faber, 1966)

Higher expectations on the part of couples, however, are not the only differences between marriage today and in the past. In the first place the number of marriages has declined and cohabitation instead has become commonplace. For this reason the number of children born out of wedlock has increased dramatically, and so has the number of schoolgirls having babies and undergoing abortions. One-parent families are obviously on the increase and divorce no longer has any stigma attached to it.

These bare facts often mask other elements. There is a general consensus that marriages between couples aged under twenty-one are more vulnerable than others. Not only do such couples have to adjust to married life, but to the fact that neither of them is yet mature as an individual. Through the normal processes of growth and development, each of them is likely to be a very different person within a few years. If such married couples also have to cope with poor housing and poor economic prospects, this will immediately place a strain on the marriage.

Difficulties between young married couples are sometimes further increased if they come from vastly differing backgrounds, religions, ethnic groupings and cultures. Compatibility of temperament between two people contemplating marriage is a matter which requires careful consideration long before a commitment is made by either. Men and women who are, for example, alcoholics, gamblers, drug abusers, violent, lacking in a sense of humour, obsessive or uncommunicative are not likely to change with marriage. Compatibility does not, however, mean having identical views; it is much more a matter of possessing the qualities of patience and tolerance.

Right from the start there needs to be a basic freedom of decision for each party within the marriage. Coercion, marriage on the rebound, or marriage viewed as a means of escape from an unhappy situation or a personal problem of some kind, are all recipes for disaster. Companionship, communication and utter truthfulness flourish best in freedom. In the case of C.S. Lewis's wife, her ability to listen carefully to whatever her husband had to say and at the same time voice her own views was remarkable. Lewis wrote:

> Her mind was lithe and quick and muscular as a leopard. Passion, tenderness, and pain were all equally unable to disarm it. It scented the first whiff of cant or slush; then sprang, and knocked you over before you knew what was happening. How many bubbles of mine she pricked! I soon learned not to talk rot to her unless I did it for sheer pleasure ... of being exposed and laughed at. I was never less silly than as H's lover.
>
> (*A Grief Observed*, Faber and Faber, 1966)

SEXUALITY

In the area of sexuality there needs to be utter frankness between husbands and wives and the ability to articulate difficulties. Here, according to Dr Jack Dominian, it is not permissiveness so much as the trivialization of human encounter which is the danger. Dominian writes passionately about how this trivialization in the name of freedom 'encourages the minimum engagement with the maximum haste, and the maximum disengagement, as in pre-marital experimentation and divorce.' Dominian goes on to argue that,

> The crisis of love lies in the fleeing from one human being to another in an attempt to find wholeness and fulfilment instead of engaging fully and overcoming the obstacles of relationship through commitment, faithfulness and permanency. Love cannot be found in the transient, the superficial and the shallow.
>
> (*Proposals for a New Ethic*)

For this reason Dominian advocates a recognition of the place of chastity within marriage, not because chastity and sexuality are opposed, but because the Church believes that such things as continence, chastity and self-control are 'a positive and creative element in Christian living.'

Provided, however, two people have genuinely prepared for marriage, many of the difficulties associated with marriage are surmountable. In such a marriage the couple are able to impart to their children what it means to enjoy a loving relationship, including the place within it of intimacy, fidelity, compassion, forgiveness, basic communal living and fulfilment. It is for this reason that parents are often described as the first and chief educators of their children in the ways of faith, not least concerning the person of Jesus and his commandments of love.

INDISSOLUBILITY AND CONSECRATION

When we are reminded that marriage for the Christian is for life, or indissoluble, we quickly realise that the gifts of stamina and perseverance are vitally necessary. This is especially important at critical times in a marriage such as the birth of children and occasions of conflict, stress and tragedy. Indissolubility is difficult to maintain in contemporary society if it is viewed simply as a law of the Church. It does take on significance, however, if it is compared with the life-long love of a parent for a child and particularly with God's never-ending and always forgiving love for us.

In a similar way procreation needs to be viewed within the context of a man and woman consecrating their lives to each other in marriage. Consecration does not mean, however, living solely for each other or even just for the children resulting from such love, otherwise such a union would contain the often hidden seeds of selfishness and the desire not to share God's gifts with others. In such an atmosphere the marriage can become the antithesis of the happiness and fulfilment to be found in the service of others.

This was very much brought home to me a few years ago when I was seated on a plane next to two businessmen. For over an hour they spoke to each other about new technologies, methods of expanding their multinational company, mergers, takeover bids and profit-making. Sitting next to them I could not help but hear their conversation and, after a while, I ventured to interrupt them.

Introducing myself to them as a priest, I asked if I might put a question to them and, when they nodded in a mystified way, I asked them why the Church as a corporate organisation was making little or no impact on the activities they were discussing.

The businessman next to me curtly replied that the explanation was quite simple. 'It is because the Church is irrelevant,' he said. 'Is it?' I asked. 'What about the Church's concern for social justice? Doesn't the Church have something to say when families in our society might be the owners of two houses, two cars and living almost luxurious lives when others are unemployed, deprived and possibly homeless, to say nothing of the millions starving in the Third World? In these circumstances, shouldn't we be at least giving to those without from our surplus?' I asked.

'Actually,' he replied, 'you are talking about me. I have a wife and two teenage children. We have two houses and five cars between us, and I regard these as necessary incentives for me to work the hours I do. Without these material benefits I wouldn't bother.

Furthermore, I'm not in the least interested in any people other than my family.'

This exchange on the aeroplane left me extraordinarily sad. Clearly the businessman had not learnt that authentic love within a marriage is always more than simply concentrating on one's partner and immediate offspring. I couldn't help wondering what would become of him should any tragedy deprive him of his wife and children. I also remembered the words of Eric Fromm in *The Art of Loving*: 'If a person loves only one other person and is indifferent to the rest of his fellow men, his love is not love but a symbiotic attachment, or an enlarged egotism.' In other words I had encountered an attitude towards love and marriage which was the complete antithesis of everything a Christian believes about them; an increasingly common attitude in our secularised society.

Marriage is perhaps the oldest and most universal form of covenant relationship that exists between man and woman. In other words, it has existed ever since creation and the time in Genesis when we first heard how 'A man leaves his father and his mother and cleaves to his wife, and they become one flesh' (Genesis 2:24).

At its best, it is for us all our first experience of love; that which we witness between our parents and that which we receive and give to them. In that sense it is also for us a school of love. The lessons we learn as members of such a school are crucial for the rest of our lives.

THE WEDDING FEAST AT CANA

It is no accident that St John in his Gospel employs a miracle at a wedding banquet to demonstrate the power of the Risen Christ and God's relationship with his people. In this story we are deliberately given no idea who the bride and bridegroom were, why they were getting married, or how they felt about getting married. To speculate on these factors, however, is to miss the point entirely, for the wedding feast is a story replete with the kind of symbolism used by and beloved of first-century Christians. It is significant that there were not many symbols more likely to capture the minds and hearts of John's readers than that of a wedding.

Not only were the Jews familiar with the notion of God as a bridegroom and Israel as a bride, but they had always believed that a banquet would inaugurate the Kingdom of God after the arrival of the long-awaited Messiah. For St John to have a wedding banquet at the beginning of his Gospel is therefore another way of announcing that Jesus is the Messiah.

It is no accident too that the mother of Jesus is mentioned as being present. To those who understood the symbolism, Mary firstly represented the Judaism of the Old Covenant from which Jesus took his humanity, and secondly she stood for the dynamic Church of the New Covenant which had replaced the covenant with Israel. It is for these reasons that Mary is described as urging obedience to Jesus' commands and says, 'Do whatever he tells you' (John 2:5). Even the word 'servant' used by John in this account for those waiting at table is not the usual word, but that which means 'deacon' or one whose task is to distribute bread and wine. Moreover, throughout the story as told by John, there are contrasts made between what he thought of as the sterile Judaic expectation of a messianic banquet and the fullness which Christ had brought. Even the jars of water in the episode are intended to represent Judaic law which, when miraculously changed into wine, symbolise the Christian eucharist. Perhaps most important, however, is the fact that the miracle at the wedding feast at Cana is the first of the seven signs John gives in his Gospel to demonstrate that Jesus is the Son of God and Saviour, knowledge vital to those who wish to attempt to follow Jesus and thereby discover that loving others in the form of service is the essential way of attaining true happiness and fulfilment.

NINE

DEATH AND BEREAVEMENT: A TESTING OF LOVE

Recently a former pupil of mine called Tom died suddenly and unexpectedly whilst travelling in India on his gap year. Intelligent, full of promise, gifted and looking forward to going to university on his return, his death came as a devastating blow to his family, friends and indeed to all of us who knew him. It was as though part of each of us died when Tom died and in the following weeks the nearest I got to finding any consolation for my inner emptiness was in the words of Marjorie Pizer:

The splendid youth is dead and is no more,
And who shall comfort those who are left?
Who shall comfort the mother who has lost her son?
Who shall comfort the sisters who have lost a brother?
Who shall comfort the friends who have lost a friend?
And who shall comfort the father?
There is no comfort for those who are grieving
For faith is not enough
To assuage the tearing wound of sudden death.
O let me not drown in the flood of grief
For all young men who died before their time
And for this one so newly dead.
O let me catch the raft of life again
And not be swept away
Into the darkest depths of grief and loss.

> ('Lament for Glenn', a young man of nineteen
> killed in a motorbike accident)

Not everyone responds in the same way to the death of someone they love. As the writer and journalist Victoria Ironside says:

> Bereavement works through us, rather than the other way round. Our responses are as different as our experiences: some need privacy, others need to shout their grief from the rooftops. Some find tears crucial, others find repression the answer; others still that there is nothing to repress.
>
> (*Independent,* 19 April 1996)

This is true whether the death of a loved one occurs at the end of a long and painful illness or out of the blue, as in the case of Tom. In extreme instances, such as that of the artist Dora Carrington, so great was her grief at the death of her lover, Lytton Strachey, that in despair she committed suicide.

> I dreamt of you again last night. And when I woke up it was as if you had died afresh. Every day I find it harder to bear. For what point is there in life now? . . . I look at our favourites, I try and read them, but without you they give me no pleasure. I only remember the evenings when you read them to me aloud and then I cry. I feel as if we had collected all our wheat into a barn to make bread and beer for the rest of our lives and now our barn has been burnt down and we stand on a cold winter morning looking at the charred ruins . . . It is impossible to think that I shall never sit with you again and hear your laugh. *That every day for the rest of my life you will be away.*
>
> (*Carrington, Diaries*, 12/17 February 1932)

The term 'bereavement' comes from the word 'reave' which means to ravage, rob and leave desolate and, although Carrington's experience may be extreme, there are recognised stages of bereavement which most of us pass through. The process of mourning sometimes lasts as long as two years and the bereaved usually initially experiences shock and disbelief, followed by an increasing awareness of what has actually happened, and finally acceptance of the death of the loved one.

In the immediate period after a death we may deny to ourselves that death has actually occurred and then feelings of guilt may arise. We may experience regret that we did not do more for the person when they were alive, see or speak to them more often, tell them things they would have liked to hear, or we may even think that we did not love them enough.

During the last three months of my mother's life, when at the age of ninety-two she was slowly dying of cancer, I made a conscious resolution that I would not carry any guilt after her death. So strong did I feel this that I determined to tell her all the things she had waited in vain to hear from me in the past. I told her I loved her; I thanked her for all the care she had given me during my life; and I apologised for the occasions I had rowed and quarrelled with her. When she died I experienced no guilt whatsoever and took great comfort from the words of Metropolitan Anthony of Sourozh I quoted earlier:

> With every person who dies, part of us is already in eternity. We must, if we love this person, live up to the great encounter of a living soul with a living God. We must let go of everything that was small, that was separation, alienation and estrangement, and reach out to that serenity and greatness, newness and abundance

of life into which the departed person has entered . . .

(From a speech on modern man facing death)

If, however, we do experience guilt at the death of a loved one and if it is enormous, we may engage in compensatory behaviour by pretending that the dead person had led a totally blameless life. In our guilt we may also project anger and hostility on those around us, and look for scapegoats. Even so, as Martin Israel has remarked:

Unexpressed anger is dangerous since it may recede into the depths of the psyche and precipitate a depression. Unacknowledged anger is likewise to be avoided since it may flare up into destructive hatred.

(*Mourning: the song is over but the memory lingers on*)

From possible shock and disbelief, anger and guilt, we then often move on to an increasing awareness that the one we loved has died. At the same time we may experience bouts of grief, pining and depression and become apathetic in our outlook. C.S. Lewis speaks of 'the laziness of grief' and describes his loathing of any activity that required effort following the death of his wife. Fortunately, tears can bring relief.

Finally, our mourning turns into acceptance but not forgetfulness of the death of our loved one. In the case of Tom, my former pupil, acceptance of his death gradually became more positive as I pondered the words of a poem by Brian Patten, which is based on four lines of a poem by Pablo Neruda:

Armada

How long is a man's life, finally?
Is it a thousand days, or only one?
One week, or a few centuries?
How long does a man's death last?
And what do we mean when we say, 'gone forever'?

Adrift in such preoccupations, we seek clarification.
We can go to philosophers,
but they will grow tired of our questions.
We can go to the priests and the rabbis
but they might be too busy with administration.

So, how long does a man live, finally?
And how much does he live while he lives?
We fret, and ask so many questions –
then when it comes to us
the answer is so simple.

A man lives for as long as we carry him inside us,
for as long as we carry the harvest of his dreams,
for as long as we ourselves live,
holding memories in common, a man lives.

His lover will carry his man's scent, his touch;
his children will carry the weight of his love.

One friend will carry his arguments,
another will hum his favourite tunes,
another will still share his terrors.

And the days will pass with baffled faces,
then the weeks, then the months,
then there will be a day when no question is asked,
and the knots of grief will loosen in the stomach,
and the puffed faces will calm.
And on that day he will not have ceased,
but will have ceased to be separated by death.
How long does a man live, finally?

A man lives so many different lengths of time.

Even so, although we may eventually come to accept
the death of a loved one, the problem of trying to
comprehend the significance of death in our lives
remains. For many there is the understandable fear
that death is equivalent to perpetual extinction for
themselves and those they love. It is here that faith
and love of God are truly tested.

For the Christian confronted with death there is
considerable comfort to be found in the Orthodox
Church's view of death and burial and especially in
the Orthodox burial service. This is based on Matins
which is a service of praise and light beginning with
the words 'Blessed is our God'. Holding candles in
their hands as symbols of the resurrection, mourners
are encouraged to take on board the idea that, though

death is fearful, it loses its power to frighten us when we view it through the resurrection of Jesus. As Metropolitan Anthony of Sourozh says:

> Death is death with all its tragic ugliness and monstrosity, and yet ultimately death is the only thing that gives us hope. On the one hand, we long to live; on the other hand, if we long sufficiently to live, we long to die, because in this limited world it is impossible to live fully. There is decay indeed, but a decay which, in conjunction with the grace of God, leads to a measure of life which otherwise we would never have. 'Death is a gain,' says St Paul (Phil. 1:21) because living in the body we get separated from Christ. When we have reached a certain measure of life – independent of time – we must shed this limited life to enter into unlimited life.
>
> (*Living Prayer*)

EPILOGUE

Twenty-nine years ago, I recall sitting truly entranced listening to a series of lectures in Rome on the subject of the Trinity, given by the French-Canadian Jesuit François Bourassa. My fellow students considered my behaviour somewhat eccentric. How could I, they asked, approach a series of mere lectures as though I were listening to a symphony or concerto by Mozart or Beethoven, looking at a picture by da Vinci or Michelangelo, or reading a sonnet by Shakespeare? How could I, they asked, be inspired by hearing such things as: 'The one God exists in three persons, sub-sistences, hypostases, who are the one divine nature, essence, substance and are equal, co-eternal and omnipotent'?

Wasn't this all celestial mathematics, they asked? And how could one properly understand this, when there exists no official definition or explanation of possible distinctions between *persona* and *hypostasis*? What, they asked, is the significance of the fact that such terms are derived from classical Greek and scholastic theology? And did I realise, they demanded, that when teaching the subject of the Trinity, one first had to ensure that one's listeners were not employing a modern definition of the word 'person'? They went on to remind me that the word 'persons' in relation to the Trinity was a way of subsuming under a general denominator what distinguishes Father, Son and Holy Spirit.

What my friends were not to know, however, was that I had been led by the lectures to the writings of the Fathers of the Church and had been reading them secretly. There I had discovered the Trinity as:

That unspeakable mystery which we worship
and which is everywhere whole and invisibly present
Father, Son and Holy Spirit,
one essence, undivided Majesty,
Splendour beyond all radiance and glory beyond all
   praise.
This the perfectly pure mind wholly surrendered
to God may in some manner perceive, but not
adequately explain: For how should it be possible to
speak comprehensively of Him who cannot be
   grasped by
the mind of a creature?

                                        (Cassiodorus)

Described like that, one is far removed from the dry as dust notions my friends were complaining of. As yet I had not encountered the writings on the Trinity by another Jesuit, Gerald O'Collins, which were to enhance greatly my understanding of the Trinity.

Then after ordination I returned to England and was sent as the junior curate to a deprived city centre parish. There lived the poorest of the poor to whom I could never talk of the Trinity in the scholastic terms my friends and I had argued about in Rome, nor would it have been appropriate for me to have used the language of the Fathers. But what was wonderful was that the parishioners there knew intuitively what the Fathers meant. Their practice of the Christian faith had given them an understanding of the Trinity through processes I had neglected.

In that parish I learnt to worship and pray to the Trinity, as distinct from employing metaphysical arguments. It was there that I searched for adumbrations or glimpses of the doctrine of the Trinity in the Scriptures. Encouraged by the people of that parish, I began to approach the Trinity in the context of the history of salvation.

With the people there I discovered the sacraments to be a participation in the eternal Trinitarian liturgy of heaven, where celebration is wholly communion and feast. Such a liturgy as is described in the Book of Revelation: 'A throne stood in heaven, with one seated on the throne: the Lord God.' Then the Lamb 'standing as though it had been slain'; Christ crucified and risen, the one high priest of the true sanctuary, the same one 'who offers and is offered, who gives and is given.' Finally it presents 'the river of the water of life . . . flowing from the throne of God and of the Lamb', one of the most beautiful symbols of the Holy Spirit. And, recapitulated in Christ, there are those who surround the throne, such as heavenly powers, all creation, the servants of the Old and New Covenants, the New People of God, especially the martyrs, the Mother of God, and finally a great multitude from every nation, tribe, people and tongue. Dimly, but with reverence, I began to discover (or was I discovered by?) the Trinity who is a God who communicates himself to us and at the same time remains the Sovereign, the Incomprehensible, Mystery.

Amid poor people, with little education but deep faith, I was taught to ask what Moses had asked the Jews, namely, 'Was there ever a Word so majestic, from one end of heaven to the other?' It was among such humble people that I learnt the meaning of what it is to follow Christ, a truth recently described by Pope John Paul II:

> Following Christ is not an outward imitation, since it touches man at the very depths of his being. Being a follower of Christ means becoming conformed to him who became a servant even to giving himself on the Cross (cf. Phil.2:5-8). Christ dwells by faith in the heart of the believer (cf. Eph. 3:17). This is the effect of grace, of the active presence of the Holy Spirit in us.
>
> (*Veritatis Splendor*)

It was there as a pastor that I began to discover the truth of Albert Schweitzer's dictum that true happiness is found only by those who seek and find how to serve. Most of all, it was in that parish that I first began to understand in practice the doctrine of deification.

According to Irenaeus, the second-century bishop and saint, deification (*theosis*) is the goal to which all Christians should aim, for it involves a 'participation (*metoche*) in God' himself. 'If the Word is made man, it is that men might become gods.' Other Fathers of the Church taught the same doctrine. Origen, for example, was of the view that the spirit is 'deified by that which it contemplates', and Basil described a human being as a creature who has received the order to become a god. Athanasius spoke of humanity's deification through the vision of God and St John of Damascus said that humanity was created for deification. St Gregory of Nyssa remarked that God created us as not simply spectators of his power, but as participants in his very nature. Although this belief is emphasised in all Eastern Orthodox teaching and spirituality, it is also to be found wonderfully displayed in the *Confessions* of St Augustine where he remarks:

> When first I knew you, you lifted me up so that I might see that there was something to see, but that I was not yet the man to see it ... And I knew that I was far from you in the region of unlikeness, as if I heard your voice from on high: "I am the food of grown men: grow and you shall

eat me. And you shall not change me into yourself
as bodily food, but into me you shall be changed."

The basis of the doctrine of deification lies in the
belief that we are made in the image and likeness of
God, the holy Trinity. For just as the three Persons
of the Trinity 'dwell' in one another in perpetual love,
so we are called to 'dwell' in the Trinity. This is what
Jesus prayed for in St John's Gospel before going to
his passion and death. Deification is also explicitly
referred to in the famous text from the Second Letter
of Peter: 'Through these promises you may become
partakers of the divine nature' (1:4).

Deification is not, however, something reserved for
a specially chosen few, but is intended as a goal to be
aimed at by all Christians. It is also attained not by
any extraordinary way, but by pursuing the everyday
process of love outlined in this book. Ultimately those
who achieve this are characterised by their serenity,
the source of which is, as John Dalrymple tells us,
their immediacy with God.

In the heart of their being they face God and
abandon themselves to him. They are not pre-
occupied with 'prayer', only with God. He
occupies them fully, because he now appears as
the Reality of all realities. They recognise that the
initiative is no longer with them, but with God.
They no longer seek him out, because they have
found him. He will never leave them, and they
know they will never leave him. In the ground of

their being they sink and merge with God. They are no longer two presences: God to them, they to God: but one presence only, a mutual immediacy.
(Costing Not Less Than Everything)

The closer we attain deification, the greater glory we give to God by becoming 'fully alive'.

FURTHER READING

Boulding, M. (ed.), *A Touch of God* (SPCK, 1982)

Brooks, P. (ed.), *Christian Spirituality. Essays in Honour of Gordon Rupp* (SCM, 1975)

Buber, M., *I and Thou* (J. & T. Clark, 1970)

Collins, P., *Spirituality for the Twenty-first Century* (Columba Press, 1999)

Dalrymple, J., *Costing Not Less Than Everything* (DLT, 1991 edn)

Fromm, E., *The Art of Loving* (Unwin Hyman, 1988 edn)

Leech, K., *Soul Friend* (DLT, 1994 edn)

Lossky, V., *The Mystical Theology of the Eastern Church* (James Clarke & Co., 1957)

Merton, T., *Elected Silence* (Hollis and Carter, 1949)
   No Man Is An Island (Image Books, 1967)
   Seeds of Contemplation (Anthony Clarke, 1972 edn)

Metropolitan Anthony of Sourozh, *Living Prayer* (DLT, 1990 edn)

Moltmann, J., *Experiences of God* (SCM, 1980)
   Jesus Christ in Today's World (SCM, 1994)

Nicholl, D., *Holiness* (DLT, 1981)
   The Beatitude of Truth (DLT, 1997)

Nouwen, H., *Intimacy* (Harper & Row, 1969)

Rolheiser, R., *The Holy Longing* (Doubleday, 1999)

Sheldrake, P., *Befriending Our Desires* (DLT, 1994)

Smith, C., *The Way of Paradox* (DLT, 1987)

Vanier, J., *Community and Growth* (DLT, 1982 edn)
   Man and Woman He Made Them (DLT, 1985)

Whitaker, A. (ed.), *All in the End is Harvest* (DLT, 1991 edn)

Williams, R., *The Wound of Knowledge* (DLT, 1990 edn)